Women in H

WOMEN
IN HARD HATS

Building Leadership, Confidence, and Life
Satisfaction in the Engineering Sector

JENNY BAILEY

Copyright © Jenny Bailey 2017
First published in 2017 by Baker Street Press | Melbourne
ISBN 9780994321459
Edited by Joanna Yardley
Cover design by Kate Durack

National Library of Australia Cataloguing-in-Publication entry
Creator: Bailey, Jenny, author.
Title: Women in hard hats: building leadership, confidence,
and life satisfaction in the engineering
sector / Jenny Bailey; Joanna Yardley, editor.
ISBN: 9780994321459 (paperback)
Notes: Includes bibliographical references.
Subjects: Women in engineering.
Women engineers–Job satisfaction.
Women engineers–Employment.
Engineering–Vocational guidance.
Other Creators/Contributors:
Yardley, Joanna, editor.
Dewey Number: 331.482

Every effort has been made to trace (and seek permission for use
of) the original source of material used within this book. Where the
attempt has been unsuccessful, the publisher would be pleased to
hear from the author/publisher to rectify any omission.

Women deserve to be able to choose engineering as a legitimate career option with the expectation that they will be treated with respect and dignity, and be free from discrimination based on their gender, to enable them to achieve their full potential.

Equally, our organisations, industry and community deserve to be able to draw upon the best engineering talent regardless of gender, and within a culture of equality and inclusiveness.

CONTENTS

DEDICATION

I dedicate this book to

- those upon whose shoulders we stand; the women throughout history who have been discriminated against, abused physically and emotionally, and even killed, because of their gender.

- those who have stood up for women's rights, from the Suffragettes to Malala Yousafzai.

- to my grandmother and mother who raised me to believe that an education, economic independence, and career, was my right.

It is also dedicated to those women who continue to fight for women's rights, a fight that is a long way from complete.

I will be forever grateful for the opportunities presented to me as a citizen of Australia in our current time.

PREFACE

Women in the engineering sector experience a range of challenges. It can be tough being a woman in any field if they are constantly surrounded by men and held in the minority. I wrote this book to help women accelerate in engineering careers—so they can achieve their full potential and maximise their life satisfaction.

Some women lack the confidence to step up to opportunities, and others are worried about getting access to developmental opportunities, particularly if they are also trying to raise a family. Our career success depends upon being technically competent, having high levels of self-leadership and interpersonal skills, being able to run teams, and manage other people. Most people have sufficient technical skills once they have finished university, and these skills can be further developed 'on the job'. Learning the interpersonal and team leadership skills can be far more difficult, but critical to success in our career and in life.

This book focusses on providing skills to help navigate an uneven playing field and achieve career success and life satisfaction. But what's in this book for men? Gender equality is good for women; it's good for men; it's good for companies and business; and it's good for our society and communities. Companies with gender equality do significantly better than those without. Additionally, happiness is significantly higher and relationships are more satisfactory in organisations (and countries) where there is gender equality (Kimmel, 2015).

MY STORY

When I was a very young girl, my mum suggested I'd make a great kindergarten teacher. Then in high school, where I was one of the few girls studying maths, chemistry, and physics, she suggested I get a degree in engineering. I didn't really know what engineering was, but the only other alternative I saw at the time was to do a degree in science—given the fact that I was smart, and good at maths and science. (I was actually lousy at writing, and managed only 53 per cent in HSE English).

I had no concept of what a degree in science might lead to. I assumed I'd be a science teacher, and I couldn't think of anything worse—so I chose engineering. The highlight of studying was attending Melbourne University and staying at Janet Clarke Hall, one of the residential colleges. I'm so grateful that my parents facilitated this for me, as it enabled me to leave home and fully enjoy university life.

At the time, 15 per cent of engineering students were women. This didn't particularly worry me as I'd just been through my final years of high school where I was one of the few girls studying maths and science. Getting my engineering degree wasn't too taxing, and I spent the majority of my lectures chatting to my friends—I was once evicted from the chemistry lecture hall for talking, and it was big enough to accommodate several hundred students and was several stories high.

I had actually chosen to study agricultural engineering. I'd grown up on a hobby farm and I loved nature and the environment. I was an early member of the Australian Conservation Foundation. At the time, environmental sciences and environmental engineering were not recognised disciplines. My agricultural engineering degree eventually morphed into the environmental engineering degree.

My first job was in the graduate program at the Melbourne Metropolitan Board of Works (MMBW). It was a bureaucratic institution and was accountable for water supply, sewage services, and drainage in Melbourne. I started in the drainage division, and was accountable for preparing the designs of drainage systems for the large waterways in Melbourne. At the time, I felt I was in over my head and had no idea what I was doing. I wanted to ask questions but didn't want to annoy my bosses and co-workers.

I was asked to design the shape of the islands and the wetlands at Lillydale Lake in Melbourne's east. My colleague was detailing the hydraulic designs, spillway, and culvert designs. Lillydale Lake is actually a retaining basin designed to prevent flooding of the town of Lillydale. The stream catchment in the significant areas of unsewered areas were reliant on septic tanks, so there was a large nutrient load coming into the lake.

The local council wanted to incorporate the lake as part of the retaining basin for local amenity. The wetlands were one of the earliest attempts, at the time, at using wetlands to filter out nutrients through reed beds. I had no idea how to design islands, and there was no instruction manual, but if you look at the Google Maps of Lillydale Lakes, the shapes of the islands exist as they do thanks to what I dreamed up on the drawing board.

I left MMBW after 18 months to pursue work in the private sector, where I worked for a small engineering consultancy called Fisher Stewart. I was their first female engineer. I was now in a profession where only one per cent of practitioners were women, and I was finding the environment much tougher then my previous role. I spent each day, alone, designing drainage systems for a subdivision in Clifton Springs, and I was going crazy. In Myers-Briggs terms, this was ISTJ (Introverted, Sensing, Thinking, Judging) work, and I was an ENTJ (Extroverted, iNtuitive, Thinking, Judging). I decided I couldn't stand engineering, and I didn't want to be an engineer.

By this stage, I was preparing for an overseas trip, so I decided to forgo engineering, and travel (with my now husband, David) to Europe. We purchased bikes in London and started on a cycling adventure. Five months into the trip, I fell off my bike and broke a bone in my foot, which put an end to our cycling trip.

We made our way back to the UK and commenced looking for work. I was incredibly fortunate to discover that thanks to Britain joining the EU and Margret

Thatcher privatising the water system, there was a significant volume of work available in the water business. I landed a job in Bath with Wessex Water. Even better, my role was with the feasibility team doing high-level feasibility studies for upgrading sewage treatment plants around all the districts—I loved it. I never wanted to do a detailed piece of design engineering again, but the big picture stuff was awesome.

On returning to Australia, I was hired as an environmental engineer, first with AGC Woodward-Clyde and then with Sinclair Knight Merz. At the same time, I studied a graduate diploma in Environmental Science. In Perth, I gained exposure to mining, and the oil and gas industry. Mining was awesome. I loved visiting the sites; I loved the size and the excitement of the mining operations. The Pilbara, in Western Australia, is one of the most beautiful places I'd ever visited.

During my time in Perth, I was sent to Thevenard Island, off the North West Shelf. It housed a small processing facility and I was there to undertake a waste audit. It is one of the most special places I've ever visited; it felt like my own tropical island. Back then, the field of environmental management was only just taking off, so I got to invent my own way of doing things.

By this time, I knew I wanted to work in the mining industry, and was lucky enough to land a job back in Melbourne with CRA, which then merged with RTZ to become Rio Tinto. I was a Principal Environmental Consultant, traveling around mine sites and facilities performing environmental audit and environmental impact statements for new operations. The environmental field was my passion. I loved the fact that it covered so many disciplines and brought them together in the environmental impact assessments.

I left Rio Tinto to study an MBA at Melbourne Business School—another highlight of my career—after which I secured a role as a manager at Yarra Valley Water in the east of Melbourne. Within twelve months, I was offered the role of Acting General Manager of Strategy and Communications. This was my dream job, and Yarra Valley Water was the best organisation I'd ever worked in. It was full of people who were community-minded and just wanted to be the best that they could be, without playing political games.

I'll be forever grateful for Peter Harford and Tony Kelly who gave me that opportunity. It was at Yarra Valley Water that I learned about leadership and organisational culture, and where I realised that my passion was enabling organisations to be highly effective through the way they were designed, structured and operated.

There were two women on the executive team, Anne and myself. (Anne was the head of HR). I admired my male colleagues and never felt discriminated against based on gender. However, there was many a time when I felt incredibly lonely, and where my perspectives were so different from my colleagues that I was uncomfortable to share them. Some of these feelings were, no doubt, based on being female in a male-dominated team.

During my time at Yarra Valley Water, I took leave to have my son, Rhys. After eleven months, I returned to the role of General Manager of Customer Operations. I worked full-time, while my husband took a year off to look after our son. That first year back was extraordinarily difficult. Although I didn't appreciate it at the time, I was exhausted. When Rhys was three, I left Yarra Valley Water—the organisation I dearly loved—because I wanted new opportunities. Ideally, I wanted to be CEO of Yarra Valley Water, but I knew it would be a long time before that role became available.

I began working at KPMG as Associate Director of Climate Change, Sustainability and Water. At the time, KPMG made significant efforts to accommodate women and introduce part-time work. I negotiated a four-day week. However, Friday, my so-called day off, became a day of nightmares; I would care for my three-year-old son while incorporating extra work for a KPMG partner who had little respect for working women with young children. Eventually, I put Rhys into childcare—on my day off, bizarre as that sounds.

After leaving KPMG, I went through a dark period in my career. Once Rhys started school, I applied for general management roles in the government sector and had three separate experiences where I felt I was discriminated against based on being a mother. After failing to re-enter the workplace as an employee, I established Parent Central, a business that teaches parenting skills, and I developed a leadership coaching practice.

I expanded my business to commit to developing outstanding female leaders in the field of engineering. I provide speaking, coaching, mentoring and training in communications, confidence and leadership to women in engineering. I wrote this book to support women who work in the engineering sector.

Chapter 1

STATUS OF WOMEN IN ENGINEERING

WHY ARE THERE SO FEW WOMEN?

There are three key reasons for the low number of women in the engineering profession. First, there is a small number of women studying maths and science at school—a trend that is getting worse. Second, only a small number of women choose to study engineering; and third, there is a relatively high dropout rate of women who do actually enter the profession. Clearly, low numbers of women studying maths and science at school is a problem for more than the engineering profession, and this needs to be addressed. It will remain difficult to attract women to study engineering while engineering is a harsh environment, particularly for women. Marlene Kanga reported that 50 per cent of women over 50 years of age who work in the sector have experienced discrimination. Running a campaign to attract women to study engineering is like inviting people to a picnic on top of an ant's nest. To address gender balance the focus needs to be on making the sector a more attractive environment for everyone, but particularly for women.

THE STUPID CURVE

The stupid curve was a term coined by former U.S. Deloitte boss, Mike Cook, in reference to the representation of men in leadership positions, and the underrepresentation of women. Given that women are equally, or even slightly overrepresented, as university graduates, and grossly underrepresented at the senior executive level, there is a hell of a lot of wasted female talent. There are strong indications that the men sitting in many of these leadership positions are not as capable as the women who have disappeared, or not travelled through the pipeline toward senior leadership positions.

The gross underrepresentation of women in the engineering sector is evidence that the sector is *dumbed down*. Assuming that intelligence is distributed evenly among men and women, then there is a significant number of intelligent women who are simply not being attracted into the sector. For example, only 14 per cent of women complete engineering degrees. Attracting more female talent to the sector would lead to a higher performing sector.

The majority of the arguments that women are not interested in nor suited to engineering fall away when we look other cultures. In India, Latvia, and Bulgaria, nearly 30 per cent of engineering graduates are women. I'd like to propose further that the 14 per cent of women who do graduate from engineering degrees are among the cream of engineering graduates. You have to be extraordinary to survive a difficult degree when you are a part of a minority. The majority of the infrastructure, teaching, and learning staff are men and not women. Graduates transitioning to the workplace need to be exceedingly gritty and determined to survive. In addition, women's orientation towards relationship and social skills combined with the analytical skills that come from being trained as an engineer should make them perfect for leadership roles in the engineering sector. Based on the number of females who graduate, female engineers should be over-represented in senior leadership roles in the sector. Clearly, they are not. A quick search on the composition of the executive teams of leading engineering firms will testify to the virtual absence of female executives.

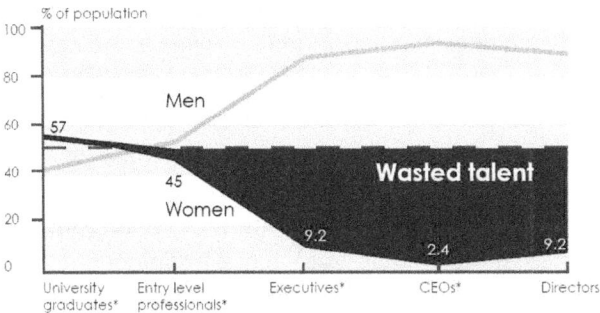

* Source: EOWA Analysis 2012 ASX500 + Mc Kinsey Women Matter Asia 2012

DOES IT MATTER?

A skilled engineering workforce underpins the strengths of economies worldwide, and women in engineering matters for the economy and for the sector.

'Increasing women's workforce participation is a game-changer, says one of Australia's top engineers. Australia lags in policies that support professional women, especially in the critical family formation years.' — Marlene Kanga

The Grattan Institute recognises that increasing women's workforce participation should be one of the top three economic reform priorities for Australia, and estimates that increasing to just six per cent of female participation would add $25 billion, or one per cent, to Australia's Gross Domestic Product (GPD) (Kanga, 2016)

WHAT DOES THE DATA SAY?

First, only 14 per cent of graduates entering the engineering sector are women, and only 12 per cent of the engineering workforce is women (Engineers Australia, 2016). If the sector was attracting the best quality talent, which comes from both genders, then 36 per cent of talented female graduates are missing.

Only 12 per cent of engineers are women and only one per cent of Australian-born female engineers remain in the industry until aged over 50 (Kanga, 2016). Only 51.2 per cent of women with engineering qualifications actually work in the engineering sector, implying that half of the women who graduate as engineers have chosen, for one reason or another, to exit the industry. There are only 176 women, compared to 5,000 men who are Fellows or Honorary Fellows of Engineers Australia, so the small numbers of women who *do* enter the industry are not making it to senior positions.

As the time of writing this book, there were 24 Managing Directors of water businesses in Victoria—of whom only one is a woman. Additionally, 24 per cent of women report sexual harassment in the workplace, and 35 per cent report discrimination, which is twice the rate of discrimination reported by men. Engineering workplaces are harsh environments, with high rates of bullying and harassment. The discrimination rate increases with age. Fifty-five per cent of women aged over 50 report discrimination, three times the rate of men in the same age group. The rates for bullying, discrimination and harassment are unacceptably high in the whole industry, and women suffer much higher rates than that of their male colleagues (Kanga, 2014)

WHAT FEMALE ENGINEERS ARE SAYING

In July 2016, I rolled out a short survey to engineers in different industries. I was interested to know whether women were satisfied with their careers in engineering. Did they have development opportunities? And were their careers, or lives, impacted by gender discrimination in any way?

My research concluded that female engineers are incredibly tolerant people. On a scale of 5, they rated career satisfaction a 3.8; development opportunities a 3.5; the culture of their existing organisation a 3.8 (where 5 was a 'great place to work'); and flexibility a 3.9. However, when I asked whether they have been discriminated against based on gender, only 13 per cent answered *no*. Twelve per cent experienced bullying or unwanted sexual advances. A further 12 per cent answered they felt unwelcome in their workplace, and

51 per cent claimed minor discrimination. In total, 87 per cent experienced discrimination to some degree, based on their gender.

When asked whether their careers had been impacted by gender discrimination, only 27 per cent answered *no*. What was interesting, however, was the significant difference between women who had children and those who did not. Forty per cent of women without children felt that being a woman had not impacted their career, where only 17 per cent of women with children felt their career had not been impacted. That is, 83 per cent of women with children felt that being female and being a mother had limited their career opportunities.

From my survey, I concluded that:

- Significant proportions of females are experiencing gender discrimination and can feel unwelcome in their workplaces.

- More than half of women without children feel that their career prospects are being impacted by their gender.

- Most female engineers, who are mothers, feel that their career prospects are being impacted.

Here are some quotes from some of the female engineers surveyed. *(The results of the survey are presented in Appendix A.)*

Things are great now; however, in my opinion, 20 years ago there weren't as many opportunities for women in engineering.

One of my first experiences as a new graduate was walking across the shop floor and hearing the site manager say to a colleague: 'I wouldn't mind putting that across my knee and spanking it'.

As a new graduate, I was the only female of three new employees who needed to be allocated to three different roles. I was given a desk role and the other two graduates (men) were mostly put on site roles. I was told they chose based on whom they felt was most suited to the role, but I felt my gender played a big part in that. Having said that, I was the first female engineer the company had ever hired and I believe that actually helped me get the job in the first place, because there were over 90 candidates that applied, and only two were women.

Passive discrimination, not being considered for the responsibility of a difficult job. Being pushed gradually towards the 'soft' roles of organising the lunchtime seminar series.

There is a noticeable two-tiered culture between the male and female consultants. Opportunities, which were commonly offered to my male counterparts, were rarely offered to women with similar experience or expertise.

The hardest thing has been taking on leader posts, since I cannot work 24/7 due to responsibilities within my family. My male colleagues do not have that problem, since their wives are taking the biggest responsibility at home. I'm in a much more equal relationship; however, my husband would never work part-time to support my career. Leadership roles, sadly, often seem to be built for persons putting family second. It should not be like that!

I'm paid substantially less than male colleagues in exactly the same role.

Career opportunities have been limited by working part-time (four days per week) after returning to work from parental leave. Actually, I'm managing a full-time job, being paid for four days per week and doing lots of work from home in my own time.

When unsuccessfully applying for a role, the feedback included, *We feel John is more capable of telling the contractor what to do—he has broader shoulders to take on the role* (with no examples of why he'd be better).

I feel out of place in all male parties.

I've worked part-time since having children, and I think this significantly impacts my progression opportunities.

At least twice at site meetings, I was assumed to be the engineer's secretary sent to take minutes.

My current company is exceptionally supportive of diversity and females in manufacturing.

I often feel like I am disrupting a 'boy's club' rather than being part of a team. There have been several incidences where I have been 'called-out' as a female and made to feel like I do not belong.

I had more issues as an electrician then as an engineer.

WHAT WOMEN CAN DO

This book is about what women can do to help themselves, while remaining true to themselves. Many women who've worked in the engineering field or in male-dominated environments have fallen into the trap of behaving like men in order to fit in. I know, because I have done it myself.

First, we must acknowledge that women in engineering are operating on an uneven playing field. The uneven playing field has 'by and large' not been deliberately designed to make life difficult for women. Given the recent history of limited rights for women, it is a wonder that it is not significantly more uneven. The uneven playing field is not the fault of men—or anyone else— it has simply evolved historically. By recognising these facts, we can give ourselves permission to accept help to navigate the uneven playing without guilt. Accepting help will go some way to making the playing field more even. Not only is learning to accept help important, but asking for help is just as important.

For many women, having a family is a huge opportunity and a joy. I'd love for women to view their time on maternity leave and raising their families as being crucially important to their personal and professional development. Being a parent is one of the best opportunities for personal development. I hope we can come to view having a family as a career, as well as a personal opportunity.

Finally, women's contribution to solving the gender equality challenge can simply be bringing their best to their work, their lives, and to the people around them. How can we, as women, be our best? How can we be catalysts for change?

WHAT'S IN IT FOR MEN?

Michael Kimmel (2015) explains why gender equality is good for men:

> Gender equality is good for countries. It turns out, according to most studies, that those countries that are the most gender-equal are also the countries that score highest on the happiness scale.

> It is also good for companies. Research by Catalyst and others has shown conclusively that the more gender-equal companies are, the better it is for workers, the happier their labour force is. They have lower job turnover. They have lower levels of attrition. They have an easier time recruiting. They have higher rates of retention, higher job satisfaction, higher rates of productivity.

> It's good for men. It is good for the kind of lives we want to live, because young men especially have changed enormously, and they want to have lives that are animated by terrific relationships with their children. They expect their partners, their spouses, their wives, to work outside the home and be just as committed to their careers as they are.

Chapter 2

GENDER EQUALITY SOLUTIONS

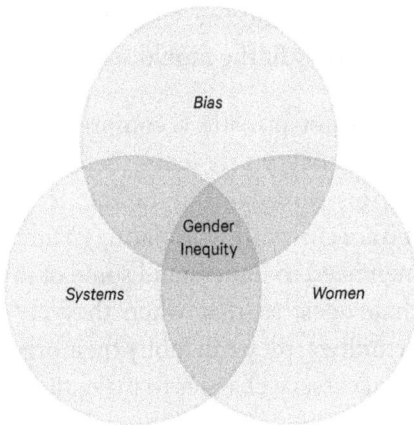

Gender Inequity Model

There is no 'silver bullet' for the problem of gender (or any other) equality issue. It is complex and requires a multi-faceted response. In business, our diversity challenge results from our belief that we operate in a meritocracy, and that Australia is an egalitarian society. The reality is that we do not, which means that we do not actually have the best people running our organisations. That, to me, is the most important issue. Imagine the increase in performance in our organisations if we really did have the best talent running them. Imagine the dramatic improvement in the social structure if people felt they were operating inside a system that was equitable and inclusive, rather than living with rejection that stems from feelings that you don't belong, or that you are somehow a second-class citizen.

When women are better represented at the senior level (as they should be), they help take their organisations towards being a meritocracy, which includes all people, whether or not they fit the mould.

This book will not provide a comprehensive solution to the gender equality problem—there has been much written on this already—but rather, it will support women who are currently negotiating an uneven playing field. Women need to understand some of the solutions to their challenges, so that when they are presented with opportunities, they can lobby their organisation to achieve the necessary changes to make the playing field more even.

We need to address three domains when looking at the gender equality challenge:

1. Bias, whether it be conscious or unconscious.

2. Systems and processes constructed with built-in biases.

3. What women must know and understand so they can be part of a solution.

BIAS

Bias is natural. It is a strategy adapted by humans to help them survive and thrive in their environment. We make judgments and assumptions in order to respond quickly to difficult situations. I was fortunate, early in my career, to receive a lesson on my own bias. My first job was with the Melbourne and Metropolitan Board of Works, and I was one of the few women there. In order to get information for costings and specifications of parts (I was designing drainage systems for Melbourne), it was necessary for me to reach the concrete pipe suppliers. I would make the call and explained in detail what I needed, only to be told I would be put through to the correct person. Over time, I noticed a pattern: women were receptionists and men were the sales engineers. To be more efficient, I would call and ask to speak to the sales engineer. (This would save me having to tell my story twice.)

One day, I called and asked to be put through to the sales engineer. The receptionist, a woman, put me through to another woman. I asked her if she could put me through to the sales engineer. She said, 'What do you want?' In my head I thought, *How annoying. I'm now going to have to explain it all to her only to be put through to the sales engineer.* I was a little impatient in my response, and said, 'Can you put me through to the sales engineer?' She said, 'I can help you.' It was only then I realised that I was actually talking to the sales engineer.

At the time, *both* of us would have been part of the one per cent of women working in engineering, but *I* had assumed that a woman couldn't possibly have been an engineer. After this experience, I appreciated that you can't blame men for assuming that I was the receptionist and not the engineer, when I had fallen into the same trap myself.

If you can ask anyone, male or female, to describe what an executive position in an Australian company would look like, the majority would envisage a white male—most likely a *tall* white male. Our ability to be biased is based on many dimensions: gender, ethnicity, height (there are not many short men in leadership positions), looks, and assumptions about sexuality. All of these biases matter. I just can't imagine how much discrimination and feelings of rejection an old black female must face in our society.

Recently, I watched a documentary about dark matter and the nature of the universe. It showed a photograph of a young female physicist, from about forty years ago, working on understanding the nature of dark matter. I said to myself, *Isn't that wonderful to see women working as physicists.* Now, probably in her early 70s, that woman was interviewed about her life in physics. I though how weird it was for me to believe that this woman, who looked like a grandmother, was *actually* a physicist, yet a man of the same age totally fitted within my expectations of what a physicist should look like.

Many organisations are putting their staff through unconscious bias training. If you search online, you can find a copy of the slide pack that Google presents to their 60,000 primarily male white employees as part of their unconscious bias training. The Diversity Walk exercise is also another tool to help understand the impact of long-term outcomes of differences in opportunity and unconscious bias.

Elizabeth Broderick developed the Male Champions of Change initiative when she was the Australian Sex Discrimination Commissioner. It is still used in Australia today. It is based on the recognition that women on their own cannot overcome the gender equality challenge. This requires men in positions of power to make changes. The Male Champions of Change initiative includes a significant number of senior men in large Australian organisations who have made commitments, and implemented actions, in order to improve gender diversity inside and outside of their organisations. It also provides a model for Male Champions of Change initiatives to run within multiple disciplines. Let's hope there will soon be a Male Champions of Change initiatives representing the engineering sector.

SYSTEMS AND PROCESSES

A multitude of systems and processes support the operation of our organisations. Many of our biases—conscious or unconscious—have been embedded in these systems and processes. Some key systems and processes must be addressed in order to help and support the goal of removing gender inequality. First, we must consider the pay gap. Many studies show that there are significant differences between salaries paid to men and women for the same job. This is often blamed on women's poor negotiating skills and the fact that women also tend to value themselves lower than men value themselves. In the past, efforts have been made to heighten a woman's negotiating skills, enabling her to better deal with pay negotiations. Again, if we're operating our organisations on the basis of being a meritocracy, this would be a non-issue.

Organisations need to understand their data and actively address discrepancies. For women, I suggest that you don't ask for a pay raise, but that you ask for your company to provide data to demonstrate that you are being paid fairly and are not being discriminated against on the basis of gender. One of the key challenges is when an organisation pays everybody differently (and keeps it a secret); this lacks transparency and contributes to the pay gap.

Second, we must address gender inequality, particularly in leadership levels, and the requirements we have for consideration of people in specific roles. Often we include requirements that exclude women, but are not necessarily relevant to the role. Christine Nixon, retired Police Commissioner for Victoria, is famous for removing *the wall*. The Victorian police force used to test their recruits for suitability for their role by asking them to scale a 1.6-metre wall. Many women failed at this step.

The need for police officers to scale a 1.6-metre high wall in the end turned out not to be a particularly important criterion for selecting potential recruits for the force. During her time on the force, Christine increased the number of sworn female officers from 14 to 28 per cent of the workforce.

Third, we must address flexibility. Not all women choose to have children, but a significant proportion do. Biases against women in the workplace are often not that visible to younger women involved in graduate programs and before they have children, but can become extraordinarily evident when they choose to have children—a massive impediment in getting women into senior leadership roles. Our goal here is not only to have more female engineers to improve the engineering sector, but to have women represented at all levels of an organisation.

Female engineers have huge potential to be high quality leaders, yet many women find themselves working outside their industries once they have chosen to start a family. I didn't actually believe the glass ceiling existed for me and my generation. After all, we were told that we were the 'pipeline of future leaders'. In my experience, the glass ceiling existed not for women, but for mothers. It was believed that mothers could not commit to their work in the way non-mothers could. This is where a lack of flexibility works against mothers and encompasses the need for part-time work and flexibility in hours worked. I feel very strongly that women (and everybody else) should recognise that the challenges of raising a family and managing the behaviour and interaction of children, in particular, toddlers, engenders a massive boost to our skill sets in getting things done, and also in our interpersonal skills.

Women returning to work after maternity leave feel they have missed a year of their journey to leadership. I want to change this perception. I want to help women and men understand that these women are returning to work armed with an impressive skill set perfected when raising their family. The need for flexibility is critical, and not just for women; but also for men who are parents, so they can contribute to raise their family and support women to maintain their careers. Finally, it is worth a brief discussion here on the case for affirmative action. Meritocracy, fairness and equality are important values for most people. As a result, many of us are uncomfortable at the idea of imposing quotas or targets for the number of women in leadership positions, or in organisations. We feel that is unfair. In addition, people will judge us negatively if we are in leadership positions, believing we are only there because of a quota and not because of our own merit.

In an article in July 2016 in *The Australian*, Peter van Onselen talked about the state of diversity in the Australian Liberal Party and contrasted that with the Labor Party, which has had a system of quotas for an extended period. He pointed out that there was zero evidence that the ALP's quota system had resulted in poor quality female candidates, and that all other efforts to improve female representation in the Liberal Party, without quotas, had clearly failed. For me, never having been a fan of quotas and affirmative action, I had to agree with Peter. The playing field is clearly uneven and it's difficult to see the glass ceiling's level of unevenness. A system of quotas and targets or affirmative action might seem unfair; but just maybe, it's levelling up the playing field.

Alex McGrath

Alex McGrath is an incredibly intelligent woman; she is well-read and wise beyond her years. Alex studied electrical engineering, as well as French and business at University, and now works as a railway systems engineer. Alex is passionate about trains, and she shares this passion with her husband, who is also an engineer and an academic.

Alex and her husband have worked in engineering industries in Europe and in various locations throughout Australia. Alex loves her work—in particular, working to a tight deadline to deliver a critical piece of infrastructure. She has done this may times in the coalfields of the Hunter Valley in NSW, where rail transport is a critical part of the regional economy.

Alex had her children early in her career; she is a mother to two boys and a girl, aged 8, 6 and 4. She currently works two days a week at Siemens. (Personally, I don't know how she does it.)

Not only can Alex design signalling systems, she can write from the heart. I believe that one day Alex will be the CEO of a large engineering organisation. Whether she achieves this goal will depend on how she can make use of the opportunities that unfold in the future.

In her own words, here is Alex describing her experiences as a female engineer.

> I sometimes wonder if I've been sold a lemon. I am a mother of three young kids, trying to have a real career in the infrastructure sector, and I don't think it's going to work.
>
> There are quite a few of us around. We are mums who are science researchers, senior lawyers, financiers, university academics, all ambitious professionals in other male-dominated fields, all of which demand an uninterrupted professional trajectory for us to achieve our ambition and potential. We just can't do it. We have kids. And our professional worlds don't give any quarter.
>
> I was caught in the trap early and missed some key warning signs. In year 12, I got perfect scores in Maths and Physics classes (in which I was the only girl). A friend's mother took me aside and asked 'What do you need to do Maths for, dear? You can't work like a man, and being clever won't help you find a husband'. I thought she was a relic of a past century or the third world, but she had a good point. In undergraduate engineering, I was one of eight women in a cohort of 300, and from the distracted way they looked at our bodies, the very existence of breasts must have been fascinating and a bit scary to many male students and even a few lecturers.

As an engineer, I've lost count of the times I needed to have a toilet specifically designated 'female' for my use. On one particularly memorable worksite, when the site manager saw me stepping out of the ute he rushed around the buildings to tear down the *girly* posters.

In general, the guys I work with appreciate my presence. They tell me the big egos aren't so powerful or aggressive with a few women around; the site language improves, and we all have a reputation for doing damn good work. They also speak up to defend me in client meetings, and invite me to play soccer with them after work. The problem with my career is not with the men I work with—it's with the structure of the industry and the companies in it.

Before our children, my husband and I both had the luxury to follow our own ambitions within the limits of our enthusiasm and ability—as most young engineers do. If there was a promotion opportunity in Newcastle or Switzerland, we could (and did) move on a week's notice. If there was a big project requiring lots of overtime, either of us could (and did) pull stupid 100+ hour weeks just for the glory of it. The problem is that this kind of work habit is expected of anyone who is 'serious' about their career.

While on my first maternity leave, I watched men, who had been graduates with me, move overseas, take promotions, and start on bigger management salaries. I went back to the same office, working only 12 hours a week, to 'help train the new grads'. Later I took on management of a small project on two 12-hour days a week (plus some work from home), expressing milk in the first-aid room between meetings, taking client calls while spotting the kids on the slide, and trying to finish documents at 8 pm on the train, while saying goodnight to the kids on the phone.

For all my effort, I still found myself working on projects, which were either so small that nobody cares, or going so badly that putting a part-timer like me on them couldn't possibly make them worse. My salary only just covered childcare and I still copped flak from my workmates about having it easy.

There are plenty of ways I could leave the engineering territory and work in some hand-wavy family-friendly job. A concerned manager once suggested, 'Maybe you'd like to run our corporate process improvement? We need a team competence manager, you'd be perfect'. But I like infrastructure projects. I like my team. I like the rhythm and the challenge of it.

I know that no matter how good I am, I will never be promoted by the conventional, sequential routes. Some days I choke on the injustice, but I still persist. This is one of many structurally sexist industries, and I have been fortunate to get the flexible working hours and professional recognition that I have.

At the same time, I have developed superpowers that apply to both of my professions—engineering and motherhood. I can tell when the 3-year-old is up to something involving sharp or flammable objects in an adjacent room, from the particular texture of the silence. I can also tell where a control system design isn't adequate, from the posture and lame excuses of the lead engineer, without even looking at a schematic.

I can cook dinner, feed the kids, hang out the laundry, answer the phone, and turn away a salesperson from the front door all at the same time. I can also write a scope of works, finish off some testing started by someone unexpectedly off sick today, rework the lab safety training procedure, and order a high-speed fibre multi-node comms system, all by 5 pm on a Monday.

I can get a sugar-high party of 5-year-olds to sit still with their hands on their heads, and persuading a room full of opinionated 50-year-old men in suits is no challenge at all.

Maybe that's why my professional world persists in being structured against mothers like me. Maybe we're just a bit too scary—

with the intellect and ambition to match the blokes, maybe even greater endurance, and who knows what mysterious Jedi mind tricks we've learned from managing young kids. One day, our kids will grow up and we will still be powerful, capable professional women. Give me another 10 years, guys. I might be CEO yet.

WOMEN'S ROLE IN GENDER EQUITY

Fulfilling your full potential

Type	Situation	% full potential	Result
Thriver	Valued and promotable	90% +	Excited
Performer	Learning and growing Career progressing	80%	Confident
Coper	Managing current role	70%	Empty
Struggler	Unfullfilled and unappreciated	50%	Unhappy
Battler	Unsustainable	<50%	Distressed

Women in Hard Hats - Achievement Model

Women are at various stages and different situations in their careers. The Women in Hard Hats Achievement Model identifies the different situations in which women find themselves. Regardless of your seniority or current circumstances, the goal is to enable every woman to achieve to her full potential.

CONFIDENCE

I've met many female engineers in my life, as a coach and an executive coach. I've noticed differences between how men and women approach their lives and careers, and I've concluded that these differences stem from a lack of confidence. Even confident women lack confidence! On the outside, they demonstrate growth and report they are doing really well, yet they often lack the confidence to step up into the next level. As a result, we see an increasing number of women in engineering, but this lack of confidence is one contribution to preventing them from achieving senior levels. We do have females in the profession, but we have few female leaders.

For example, I'm currently coaching a hugely capable woman and have started discussing how to position her for her next role. 'Aw, I'm not sure,' she repeats.

I can only assume that when women are surrounded by unsupportive messages they start to believe the same messages. The external 'uneven playing field' gets replicated inside our own belief systems.

HOW TO CURATE CONFIDENCE

There are many definitions of confidence. For the purposes of this book, I've identified what I see as three key elements of confidence that will significantly improve career advancement and life satisfaction for women in the engineering sector.

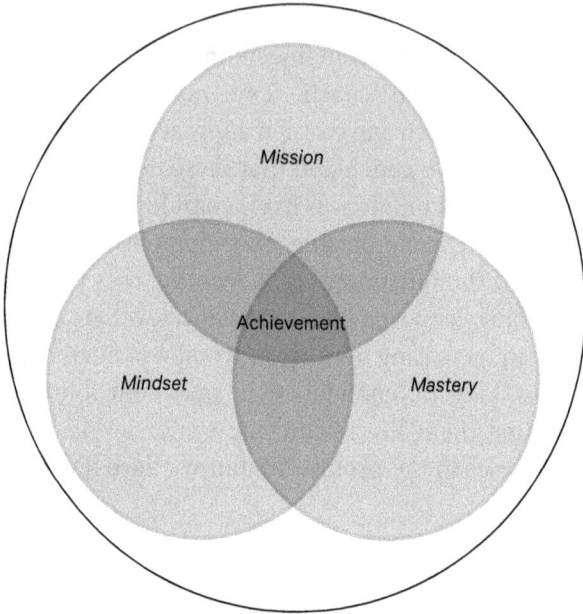

Curating Confidence Model

First, there's mission—when we understand why are we doing something. Our mission is aligned to who we are on a deeply personal level. This provides the energy to overcome obstacles. Second, there is mastery—confidence comes from knowing we have skills. Finally, the most important element is what I call mindset mastery. How do we master our thinking and mindset for success in life?

Deborah Donald

Deborah's first job was a graduate at Country Road Board (CRB) (now known as VicRoads). As with many female engineers, her husband was also an engineer.

Very early on in her career, Deborah noticed significant norms in the workplace that made assumptions about the gender of people who worked in engineering at the CRB. Deborah was an avid collector and shared with me samples of memo pads that had already pre-printed the title 'Mr'. In the CRB, phone messages were taken 'From Mr (insert surname here) to Mr (insert surname here).' Deborah pointed out to her organisation some of these assumptions, and new notepads were created. I suspect that many women (myself included) have Deborah to thank for getting some of these things changed.

Deborah started her family in her twenties; she had two daughters. One of her challenges was to persuade her employer to provide her with the opportunity to return to work on a part-time basis. The CRB's first response to this was that it was impossible, but Deborah and a female colleague, who was also in a technical position with a new baby, discovered that the New South Wales Road Board did offer their staff part-time work. These were in the pre-internet days, but Deborah managed to get a copy of HR procedures from New South Wales and shared them with the CRB

HR department. It took them eleven months to document and implement their new policy of part-time work, that applied to all staff.

On returning to work after a second round of maternity leave, Deborah took a role at the Australian Road Research Board (ARRB) and continued her career in roads. This organisation also offered the flexibility of part-time work, which Deborah found enabled her to raise her daughters and continue her career. After seven years at ARRB she applied for a part-time role at a traffic engineering consultancy, then called Andrew O'Brien & Associates, and now called O'Brien Traffic. Deborah continued working part-time until her children were well into high school.

Deborah is now Managing Director at O'Brien Traffic, which has 20 employees, including five female engineers (two of whom work part-time, as they have young families). As well as technical challenges, traffic engineering involves considerable liaison with clients, road authorities, Councils, and members of the public. For many projects, there are a number of possible solutions rather than only one right answer. Deborah often finds that female engineers work really well in this field, as they often have excellent stakeholder relationship skills.

I really appreciated Deborah taking the time to share her story with me, and also remind me and share with me the work that women have done over extended periods to make things easier for women that come after them. Deborah experienced biases that I did not encounter when I joined the MMBW, which was a very similar organisation to the CRB, only four years later.

Chapter 3

MISSION

Let's look at mission—understanding why we are doing something. Why, as females, are we working in engineering? Why are we wearing a hard hat?

Below, you will see four elements to understanding mission, at the centre of which is **purpose**. *What is your purpose in life?*

Next are our personal **values**. A successful life is one that is lived according to our core value set.

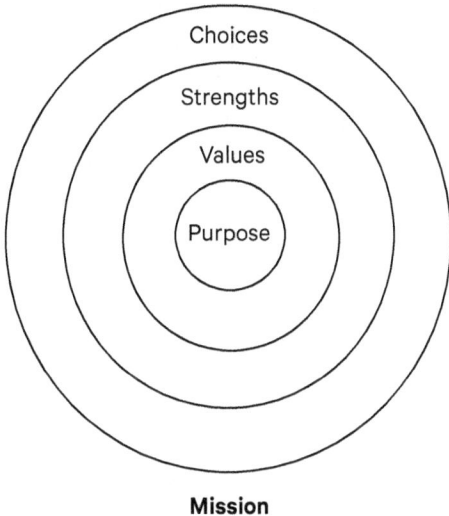

Choices

Strengths

Values

Purpose

Mission

The next element is **strengths**. Our strengths are our natural-born natural talents that we develop, grow and cultivate over time until they become real personal strengths, on which we rely to achieve our goals.

Finally, the fourth element are the **choices** we make surrounding our profession, our career, whom we choose to work with, whom we marry, and finally, as women, choosing to start a family, if that options is available.

UNDERSTAND YOUR PURPOSE

Success, in life and your career, comes when you clearly understand your purpose. Understanding your purpose and working towards it, provides enormous fuel to your energy systems that keeps you going when things look tough. It is the fuel to persistence and overcoming obstacles. Simon Sinek describes this in his famous TED Talk 'Start with Why'. Few people really understand what their life purpose is. They finished school, went to university, and got a job in the profession dictated by their degree. Decades later, they find themselves working in a job that may pay the bills but doesn't provide great interest. It soon becomes increasingly hard to get out of bed in the morning.

Often a career crisis provides us with an opportunity to re-evaluate what's really important to us. Such career interruptions might be a forced redundancy, or for women, the process of starting a family. Taking some time out to look after young children provides us an opportunity to reflect on our career to date and to think about what we really want to do with the rest of our lives.

My opportunity to work towards my purpose in life came from a career crisis. I had begun working for KPMG as Associate Director for Climate Change, Sustainability, and Water. The combination of the global financial crisis, and the government changing its mind on implementing an Emissions Trading Scheme, meant I wasn't in my new role for long and was soon out of work for the first time in my career—with a four-year-old at home.

I rested for a couple of months and thought about what I really wanted to do in life. This was a dark period for me. I didn't feel I had the energy to go back to an executive role, and I couldn't face telling my son that he would have to have a nanny again. Being a full-time mum did not appeal. I really didn't know what I was going to *do*. What was I going to do with the rest of my life? Yes, I needed economic security, but *what was I actually going to do with the rest of my life*? I had so many skills and talents, how were they going to be deployed?

I contacted a friend who was in a similar situation. She told me about a book she was reading. It was called, *I Could Do Anything I Wanted If Only I Knew What It Was* by Barbara Sher and Belinda Smith. I said to my friend, 'Wow, sounds like I need to read that book. What does it say?' Her one-line summary was 'do something'. If you don't know what to do, just do something. You never know what will come out of 'that something'. I took that advice and I enrolled myself to become an accredited instructor in teaching Dr. Thomas Gordon's *Parent Effectiveness Training*. At the time, I couldn't justify the expense and there was no clear career purpose for doing this. I certainly had no plans to teach parenting skills. However, nine months later, when I decided to start my own business (in something); I chose to teach parenting skills. I chose it because I had become so passionate about it and to this day I am incredibly proud of the positive impact on parents and their children.

For those of you wishing to understand your own purpose, I recommend Dr Stephen Covey's *How to Develop Your Personal Mission Statement*. I also love Richard Bolles' work on understanding career change in his book *What Colour is Your Parachute?*

> Your third mission here on earth is one that is uniquely yours, and that is A) to exercise the talent that you particularly came to earth to use, your greatest gift which you most delight to use B) in the places or settings that God has caused to appeal to you the most, and C) and for those purposes that God most needs to have done in the world. (Bolles, 2016)

Take the time to understand who you are, your talents, your skills, and your values. Take some time out. Invest in discovering your mission in life; hop on the train that's going in the right direction and fuel your engine to keep achieving and contributing. Stephen Covey says, *'If the ladder is not leaning against the right wall, every step we take just gets us to the wrong place faster'*.

UNDERSTAND YOUR VALUES

Values are our core beliefs or ideals. They guide our lives. Our values dictate our behaviour. If we believe that children should be seen and not heard, then we're unlikely to put much effort into listening to them. If we believe that being listened to is essential for a child to grow up with a sense of their own value, then we are far more likely to behave differently and put much more effort into listening to our children. Understanding our own values helps us make decisions that are true to us, rather than being overly influenced by the people and what they tell us we should be doing. It is worth putting some effort into understanding your values, because they will drive your behaviour—it is very difficult to find the motivation to do things that you don't value.

For example, a couple of years ago I was persuaded to set up a self-managed super fund. From a rational perspective, I thought it was a great idea to take more control over my investment and secure my financial future. However, I have done an appalling job of managing this fund. I was simply not motivated. I don't value the work of getting the governance right and researching the appropriate investments. The rational part of my brain told me it was more important to manage my super than it was to call a client. In reality, I just don't value it enough. Recognising this (and not fighting it) freed me up to make the sensible decision to pay others who are better qualified and more motivated to manage it on my behalf.

To help identify your key values, first find a list (there are many lists of values on the internet), then go through it and highlight those you identify with and that appeal to you. Then you can prioritise them: pair each value then ask yourself which ones you value higher. Continue this exercise through by pairing all of the possibilities until you come up with a ranking of 1 to 10. A useful trick for doing this is to write each of the values separately on an index card and as you pair each one with each other, you can move the higher-ranked index card up the list.

Understanding your values can help you make important decisions like career moves, organisations to work with, selecting a partner and even choosing a school for your child/ren. Although I trained as an engineer, I spend most of my life now teaching parents and helping executives improve their relationships because I value human connection and relationships where I don't particularly value detail, and I'm not particularly interested in understanding how things work. I ended up as an engineer because I was smart at school and performed well in maths and science. But I didn't value the detailed design work of an engineer. I value relationships and working with people, so for me leadership and managing people was something I dearly loved. I know I would make an terrible accountant. I don't particularly understand the details of ledgers, but there are others who enjoy it—they value it. The key to happiness and career success is to work out what you value and work in that field. Understanding your values is also critical in determining what organisations will provide you with the most enjoyment.

We enjoy working with people who share our values. My biggest career disaster came from not fully understanding the values of the organisation I was joining. I didn't share those values. As a result, I didn't like the people and I'm sure they didn't like me. Now, my family is deciding on a secondary school for my son. As we tour schools, my husband looks at the facilities while I strike up conversations with the teachers and the principal. I'm trying to understand the values of the school and of the principal because their values will dictate their decisions which, in turn, will influence my view of the school.

A discussion on values wouldn't be complete without talking about the concept of authenticity. It is easy to fall into the trap of wanting to be like someone else, but the thing is, you can't be that other person.

UNDERSTAND YOUR STRENGTHS

A successful life comes from living your life to utilise your strengths. You need to play to your strengths. 'You will excel only by maximising your strengths, never by fixing your weaknesses.' (Buckingham & Clifton, 2001).

The concept of living lives to utilise our strengths, rather than trying to fix our weaknesses was revolutionised by Buckingham and Clifton (2001), and challenges our schooling system and workplaces that endlessly focus on our weaknesses. If children are great at dancing, we send them off to do spelling. If children are great creative writers, then we tell them they're not very good at maths and make them do more. This is not to say that, at times, working on our weaknesses isn't necessary, but a truly powerful life is one that lives from our strengths. When I go for a run, I run on my legs; they're the strongest part of my body. It would make no sense to go jogging on my arms—to use the weakest part of my body for the task of running.

Strengths come from our natural talents; they are the things for which we have a natural aptitude. We develop and grow our talents into strengths. A clue to discovering your talents is to ask yourself if you are enjoying the task. When we are exercising our strengths, we are in flow. We love what we do. Warren Buffett (CEO, Berkshire Hathaway) says that one of the things that makes him special is the fact that every day he gets up and has a chance to do what he loves to do.

I have two particular strengths: one is collecting and one is learning. There is nothing I love more than learning. I collect knowledge like other people collect stamps. My bookshelves are crowded. However, my weakness is in detailed focus and specification of the tiniest detail. One of my career experiences involved spending eight hours per day locating and designing a drainage system. I didn't talk to anybody all day, and nobody spoke to me. It was one of the most torturous things I could have done. It involved every one of my weaknesses and none of my strengths.

Now I live my life according to my strengths. I collect; I assimilate knowledge and learning, and communicate that back to people in ways that change their lives. It gives me joy. It motivates me. Every day I get up and look forward to hitting my desk and getting on with my work. It gives me great pleasure, and I'm really good at it. When I'm working in this way, I'm in flow. For many people, they would hate to do what I do because they would not be playing to their own strengths.

When we recognise the importance of living life from our strengths, and we give up on hammering ourselves for our weaknesses, joy comes back into our lives. We are so much more capable and we are far more able to deliver on our life's purpose. We are defined by our strengths, not our weaknesses, and we can live from them. I believe we can radically change the world, and the world of our children, from developing a culture that's focused on strengths and not on weaknesses. I highly recommend that everybody gain an understanding of his or her strengths.

(To identify your strengths, you can do an online analysis. Go to www.gallupstrengthscenter.com)

UNDERSTAND YOUR CHOICES: THE CHOICE TO HAVE A FAMILY

A significant number of men and women are afforded the opportunity to have a family. The impact on women's careers, and life, however, is significantly greater than that for men. This is for three key reasons. First, women have to physically bear the child, carry it for nine months, and give birth. This is physically demanding, time-consuming, and the hormonal changes associated with falling pregnant, bearing children, and breast-feeding are not insignificant. Second, the hormonal drives to care for children are significantly greater for women than for men. This difference is biologically driven and difficult to change. Third, there are significant societal expectations that women must be the prime caregivers for children.

These days, we see more men picking up the childcare challenge and being significantly more involved with raising their children. Sometimes men are the primary caregivers for their children. Even in these instances, the impact of having children is still greater on a woman's career than on a man's (even in a similar situation). The question then becomes, is having a family one's sole mission in life, or is it just something we do as we travel through life?

I've spent more than four years teaching parenting skills that are based on relationship orientation rather than parenting from a place of power. As such, I have interacted with thousands of parents, both male and female, and I've met only *two* women who believe their sole purpose in life is to raise children. I believe that every parent comes to the task of parenting wanting to do the absolute best job that they can. I don't think being a parent is one's only mission in life. In my observations, the mothers who have other goals in life make fantastic parents, because they're not overly-invested in how their children turn out, because they have their own goals and successes that bring them satisfaction, and don't rely on the success of their children to measure their own self-worth and they avoid putting undue performance pressures on their children.

The choice to have or not to have children is a significant one—both of which are valid life choices. There is no doubt that having children is time-consuming, and for the majority of mothers, has a significant impact on their career, but it is something that we can do in parallel with the rest of our lives, not as a sole purpose. One of the few women I met for whom having a family was the most important thing was the mother of four children. As her youngest was growing up, it was clear that she wasn't going to have a fifth. In addition, the family finances were in a perilous state, and she had zero desire to pursue a career outside family. She chose to start a family day care centre, and to care for other people's pre-schoolers. That was her purpose in life, and I couldn't think of a better person than her to help care for other people's children.

THE CHALLENGES OF MOTHERHOOD

There are no right or wrong answers when it comes to caring for your family and maintaining your career, but I do have some suggestions. My first one is this: as a woman, it is essential to be economically independent. That doesn't mean you have to be working all the time, but you do need to know that you can get a job and earn an income if things go bad. Let's be clear and just say, a man is not a financial plan. No one gets married expecting to have that marriage break down, yet one third of marriages fail, and many of those marriages have young children involved, so maintaining employability is an important insurance policy. Putting oneself in a position of being economically weak is risky, and women are at risk because it's very easy for the woman to take on the role of parent, while the husband earns the money.

Working while caring for a young family is physically and mentally exhausting. So many women report high levels of guilt for not being with their children as much as they feel they should be, while also feeling that they are neglecting their work. Feelings of failure are common. Additionally, when mothers return to work they have been 'washed with hormones', and for the majority of us, our confidence has been depleted. We may think, *All I'm doing is working to cover the cost of childcare, what am I doing?* (I've always wondered why we matched the cost of childcare against the wife's salary and not against the husband's). So there's plenty of disincentive to keep working when your children are young, but in my observations, putting off re-entering the workplace until the children have started school—and if you have several children, this can be something like 8–10 years—only makes the transition more difficult.

I believe that hanging in there and spending all your money on childcare pays off—it ensures you retain employability and have a greater earning potential because you've maintained your career. Returning to work sooner rather than later also keeps you mentally fit. Many of us go back to work just to keep sane and to keep our brain working.

It is not anthropologically normal for one woman to take on the full load of caring for young children. We evolved from tribes and we would have had our mothers, our sisters, our cousins, and our nieces, all helping us raise a child. It does take a village to raise a child, and our children get enormous support and learning from the other adults that help look after them when they're young. I'm amazed at the number of people who insist that there's no way their children will go into childcare, and that they will care for their children themselves. I believe that these children are being disadvantaged developmentally, because childcare offers so much opportunity for emotional connection and mental stimulation. All children should be in some form of play-based childcare—let's call it early education—from two years old for some time.

So here's my tips for maintaining your career once you have a young family. Choose your organisation, one that will enable maternity leave, flexibility, and part-time work, before you choose to start your family. Then utilise the flexibility and part-time options offered to you. Pay for help, pay for childcare, and if necessary, pay for nannies, cleaners, and babysitters, so you can go out to dinner with your husband. It's essential that as a parent you're well looked after and not too exhausted, because you can't care for children if you're not in a good state yourself. I know all that seems incredibly expensive, but it's only for a short time when your children are young.

Finally, hang in there, even when the times get tough. When you have a young family, it seems like you live, breathe and sleep your children. But there is a light at the end of the tunnel when your children become more capable and independent, which enables you to then grow and develop your career and be a great role model for your children

Amanda

Amanda studied drafting when she left school. In those days, drafting was done by hand with pencil and paper on large boards. Luckily, at university, Amanda also studied CAD (Computer-Aided Design).

Amanda worked in architectural firms, which she did not enjoy as she felt they were hierarchical. She chose to go back to university and study Construction Management at RMIT. She then got a job at a university in the Property Services Department where she has been for the last 20 years. During that time, she project-managed, on behalf of the university, significant building construction projects up to the value of $130 million. Amanda found ways of managing within the adversarial contracting environment where many women would be put off by the potential for conflict without developing an aggressive personality.

Amanda has two children aged 11 and 14. Her husband also works in property management. Her employer has accommodated Amanda working part-time, particularly while her family was young; but it has always been a challenge, given that construction doesn't stop when you are not at work. So there has often been pressure for Amanda to take on more hours than she would ideally like to.

Again, as I have found with so many other women, it's not being a female that's a problem when you work in male-dominated environment—being a mum holds the challenge. Amanda currently works four days a week and every Thursday afternoon the innocent joking from her colleagues around her 'constant long weekends' are annoying for Amanda. After all, she only takes home 80% of her full-time salary, yet often finds that on her day off, she's working for no pay.

Life for Amanda is a constant juggle between parenting responsibilities and the work she loves in a contracting environment. It broke her heart one day when her son said, 'I hate your work!' Without the support from her husband, who works from home one day a week, and her parents and parents-in-law, life would be even more difficult.

Chapter 4

MASTERY

Mastery is essential for confidence. As engineers, we need to be masters of our technical skills. As employees, we also need to be masters of working effectively with others. Organisations are social units. The effectiveness of the organisation depends on the quality of the interactions between individuals within the organisation and is greatly enhanced by the effectiveness of the managers within it. As engineers, we have spent years at university and continued workplace learning, honing our technical skills. However, as employees the key to our effectiveness is mastery over our relationships and mastery in managing and leading others, social mastery. This is the focus of this chapter.

As part of developing social mastery, we'll be looking at its two dimensions: one-to-one communications, and one-to-many, and informal communications and as a manager/leader.

There are four elements, as indicated in the mastery model below: relationship skills, speaking skills, managerial skills, and team leadership skills.

	One-to-One	One-to-One
Informal	Relationship Skills	Speaking Skills
Manager/Leader	Managerial Skills	**Team Leadership Skills**

RELATIONSHIP SKILLS

Emotions and our Brain

Before we talk about communication, we need to understand the importance of emotions. Emotions make the world go around. Although we think we work and live in a rational world, most people make the majority of their decisions based on their emotions. Marketers understand this. Even if someone tells you their decision to purchase a new car was based on rational elements like cost or technical features of the vehicle, you will discover they actually chose the car based on their emotional gut-feel.

Parents, or anyone who involved with young children, learn to deal with emotions. Children are extremely emotional, because they have yet to develop the brain capacity to regulate and control their emotions. As parents, we need to learn a new language—I call it emotion-ese. We need to help our children with communicating their emotions. If we can learn to deal with the emotional meltdown of a three-year-old, we can certainly deal with any challenge presented at work.

Broadly, our brain can be considered to have three key parts. The first is the **reptilian brain.** The reptilian brain is programmed with our *fight or flight* instincts. Wrapped around the reptilian brain, is the **mammalian brain**— the emotional brain. This is called the limbic system. Humans, along with all mammals, have an emotional brain. It is because other mammals have an emotional brain that we enjoy their company (and why we love our dogs, our horses, and our cats). The mammalian brain evolved to enable us to care for our young. Reptiles, on the other hand, will eat their young, because they see an egg of a baby reptile as a food source. As mammals, we love our young, and such emotions allow us to protect our young.

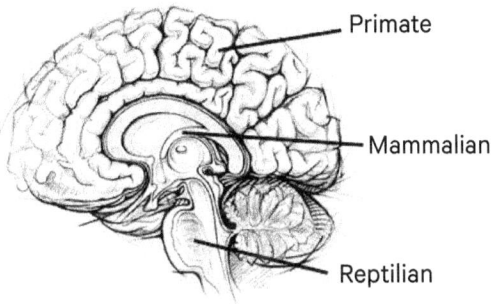

Finally, there is the **primate brain**. The primate brain is the rational part of our brain, the neocortex, is wrapped around the reptilian part of the brain. The rational part of our brain enables us to think logically, to plan, and to imagine new futures. This rational part of our brain is incredibly powerful—it makes us human.

However, when it comes to dealing with strong emotions, our brain has a design flaw. Our reptilian brain—our fight or flight responses—rather than our rational brain responds to situations when we are experiencing strong emotions. When we are upset, or angry, or frightened, our rational brain is switched off and non-functional, causing us to do things we regret later. You might ask, *What was I thinking when I did that?* and the answer is, you weren't actually thinking. Your rational brain was deactivated.

Understanding how the brain operates during times of strong emotion can help us understand other people, and enable us to communicate better with them.

When I shared this concept with a friend (that we do silly things when our rational brain switches off), she looked sheepish and confessed to me that she once gave her boss *the finger* when she was upset. I remember being on a bike ride in the UK that left me feeling absolutely exhausted. The cycling group gathered afterwards for tea and I felt hurt and left out by some of the social interaction. I threw a tantrum. My husband was mortified at my behaviour, and I still look back on that day in embarrassment. Emotions rule.

We are social beings. We cannot survive without our tribe, and being a hermit is not an option. Being socially connected with the people around us is as necessary as oxygen. Social isolation or solitary confinement is used as a punishment, and people held in solitary confinement experience a range of mental health problems, including anxiety, panic, insomnia, paranoia, aggression, and depression. Social connection is essential for our health. Social mastery is a critical skill for life success. As engineers, we spend at least four years studying the science and art of engineering, yet social mastery is critical for job success. Most of us are not trained to have good social skills. We learn the majority of our social skills in our family setting, so social ineptitude is passed down from generation to generation. We do not teach our children how to communicate their needs and feelings in a non-blameful way. No one teaches us how to listen properly to one another, and to help another person with their emotions and upsets. As a result, we're all petrified of upsetting other people. We're afraid of their sadness, because we don't want to be sad. We're afraid of their aggression and anger because it frightens us. We lack confidence in how to deal with these situations, yet, they are critical for success.

When I did my MBA, every subject required me to work with a team of strangers as part of a syndicate team. The results of the syndicate project were marked and became part of our overall final mark, and let me assure you that MBA students are obsessed with their marks. Yet the students are given no training or advice on how to run a successful syndicate team. Anxiety levels were through the roof and nobody wanted to be left holding the baby and doing all the work while their other syndicate members skived off. How different it would have been had we had good social skills.

THE IMPORTANCE OF RELATIONSHIPS AND COMMUNICATION

The quality of our relationships with other people is a critical determinant of our physical and mental health, and well-being.

'Dozens of studies have shown that people who have satisfying relationships with family, friends, and their community are happier, have fewer health problems, and live longer.'—Harvard Medical School (2010)

The quality of our relationships is also critical in the family environment. The quality of a child's relationship with its parents has a huge influence on a child's well-being and emotional development, and its ability to cope with situations, challenges, relationships and living. The key to maintaining quality relationships, and the sustenance that nurtures and grows quality relationships, is the quality of our communication with others. It is like the food we put into our bodies—it needs to be nutritious, healthy and free from toxins. There are actually only four ways to communicate with another person. In the **written** form, either we can *read* or we can *write*. We spend years at school learning how to read other people's communications and how to write and express ourselves on paper. The other mode of communication is **face-to-face** and involves either expressing ourselves through *speaking* or understanding another person through *listening* (Covey, The 7 Habits of Highly Effective People, 1989).

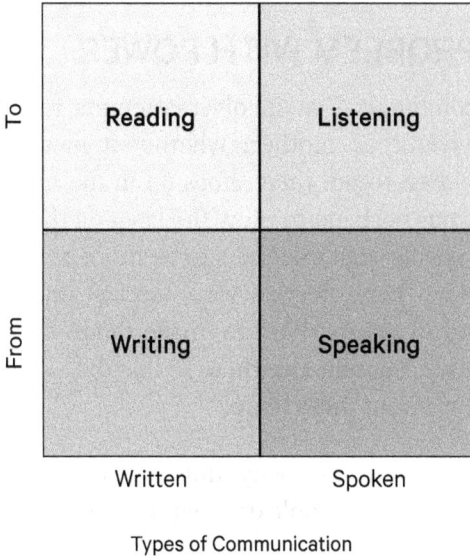

Types of Communication

The relationships between people will be negatively impacted by poor face-to-face communications. What is worse, is that we believe our face-to-face communications are accurate, and that when we say something, someone else actually understands it. In reality, only a proportion of what we are trying to communicate to another person is ever actually understood, and sometimes it is completely misinterpreted. It's like a page of text with two-thirds of the words removed and the rest of the sentences jumbled about.

Misunderstandings due to inaccurate or poor quality spoken and face-to-face communications cause tremendous problems in our relationships, and are a likely cause of the majority of marriage breakdowns.

THE PROBLEM WITH POWER

Much communication involves attempts to influence the behaviour of another: whether it means getting your children to put their shoes on in the morning, or getting your husband to mow the lawn on the weekend or getting your staff members to be more polite to your customers. There are two ways we can influence the behaviour of others. We can 'make them' do what we want, or we can influence them so that they also want to do what we want them to do.

Historically, and in many domains of our modern society, we 'make' people do what we want using power. We put our children in time-out if they don't do what we want; we give our husbands the silent treatment (or deny them sex) if they don't mow the lawn; and we demote our employees if they don't do what we want. Making people do what we want requires the use of power.

We can also 'encourage' people to do what we want though rewards like gold stars for children, cuddles and kisses for husbands and pay rises for employees. Using rewards also requires us to have more power than the other person. This is a system of punishment and rewards or often known as the *carrot and the stick*. This system requires the use of power.

Sources of power in the workplace are subtle and covert. Opportunities for using power negatively include giving a poor performance review, speaking poorly about an individual to damage their reputation, denying an individual resource or denying them flexibility, and making it difficult for others to balance their work and personal lives. On the incentive side, we can provide opportunities that might enhance careers.

A system of punishment and rewards is also a common paradigm for how we raise our children. Parents use a system of punishment and rewards because they have power over young children. We have the power to make them do what we want by using punishments, time-out, taking away privileges, and in the extreme, physical violence. Scolding or admonishing a child is another psychological punishment that is easily inflicted on children. As parents, we also have significant resources to encourage compliance. Treats, toys, chocolate frogs, praise, privilege; these are all incentives that we can use in order to encourage compliance from our children under our system of punishment and rewards, or the carrot-and-stick approach.

There are a range of problems associated with the use of power or punishment and rewards in our relationships with others. First, a system of punishment and rewards can be used only when we have power. In the workplace, a manager has some power with respect to a direct report, but many of us are without power or the authority to get things done. As parents, we run out of power when our children become teenagers. It is very difficult to 'ground' a teenager. It is very difficult to put them in time-out. Our system of gold stars and chocolate frogs, that worked so well when they were young, does not work on our teenagers.

The second problem is that every time we make someone do something against their will, we generate resentment from them. Employees resent being asked to do something when they have no context or input into that task. Children resent being made to do something they don't want to do. Using power over others damages our relationship with them. In the parent-child context, it's particularly problematic, because not only does our power run out when our children become teenagers, but there's often a bank of resentment as the child has been made to do things against their will over their lifetime. Teenagers are not actually resenting or rebelling against their parents when they become teenagers, they are rebelling against their parents' use of power over them.

Third, these systems undermine our influence. The quality of our relationship is a key determinant of the amount of influence we have over another. The use of punishment and rewards damages that relationship and, therefore, undermines our influence. It stops us getting things done at work and, at home, it prevents us from having influence in our children's lives and over their behaviour. The thing is, a system of punishment and rewards may compel or coerce somebody to do something (that is, change behaviour), but it does not influence the way they think about something.

Finally, when people are 'made' to do something they will do the bare minimum required for a task. A system of punishment and rewards undermines intrinsic motivation from an individual. 'People use rewards expecting to gain the benefit of increasing another person's motivation and behaviour, but in doing so, they often incur the unintentional and hidden cost of undermining that person's intrinsic motivation towards the activity' (Pink, 2011). The focus of modern corporations is to build 'engagement': the desire for people to want to be doing what they are doing. Greater 'engagement' equals greater performance and productivity.

The question is not whether we should use the carrot *or* the stick, as neither the carrot nor the stick is helpful to us in our relationships with other people. The carrot and the stick are two sides of the same coin and we need to reject that coin. The alternative, one that generates influence and engagement, is a system of empathy and reason, where we replace the carrot and the stick with the heart and the head. The first step towards doing this is to understand the communication square.

THE COMMUNICATION SQUARE

Once we throw out the punishment and rewards toolkit, we need to replace it with an alternative toolkit that enables us to lead from the heart and the head using empathy and reason. Such tools address each of the four quadrants in the *communication square*. The skills outlined in this square cover all of the possibilities in dealing with another person. This toolkit is applicable in all interactions with others, including parent and child, and manager and employee.

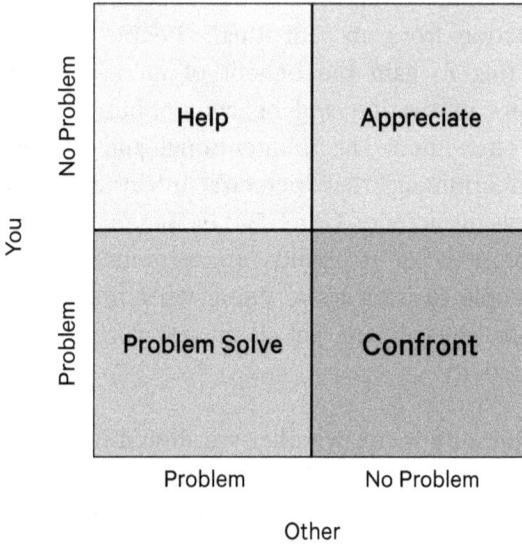

Communication Square

In our relationships with others, we are in two alternative 'states'. We may have a problem. Our needs are not being met, and we are in an upset state or we may be content, our needs are being met and we don't have a problem. The other person will also be in two alternative states.

Consider, for example, a business situation. In the top right corner, neither the manager nor the direct report has a problem. This is our opportunity to **appreciate** and strengthen the relationship with the other person using the tools of **self-disclosure.**

In the top left corner, the direct report has a problem. The goal here is to **help** the other person with their problem, and the key tool is called **active listening**. This is a tool to assist another person with their problem and with their emotions. Once we have done this, we're able to re-engage the brain and work out a rational solution to the problem.

In the bottom right quadrant, you have a problem. The goal is to **confront** the person with your problem and your key tool is an '**I-message**'. This is a way of communicating our needs to another person in a non-blameful manner so we are unlikely to elicit a defensive response.

Finally, in the bottom left quadrant both of us have a problem and our goal is to **problem-solve** using the **problem solving** method. The problem solving method draws together the skills of active listening and I-messages.

APPRECIATE

When we are in the **appreciate** quadrant, we have the opportunity to build and strengthen our relationship with the other person. We do this through self-disclosure. Self-disclosure involves sharing information about ourselves and our positive feelings towards the other person. We do this using an 'I-message' as opposed to a 'you-statement'.

For example:

'I really appreciated how you prepared such a quality report in such a short period. This enabled me to keep my boss happy. I was very relieved about this, because I know she was anxious about this report.'

Or for children:

'I really appreciated how you unpacked the dishwasher, as I'm very busy right now, having just come home from work and need to prepare dinner.'

Just sharing information about ourselves can build relationships. The more others understand you and 'what makes you tick', the better they can help you and appreciate you for who you are.

For example:

'I really enjoyed the weather on the weekend as it meant I could get out on my bike, and I love cycling.'

Or for children:

'I love it when I see you reading because I love reading too, and I hope you share this love when you are older.'

Often, in our misguided attempts to appreciate others, we tell them how great they are, *You're such a good girl. You're such a reliable employee.* People don't like being judged, and they certainly don't like to be judged negatively. Positive judgments often leave us feeling pleased on the one hand but exposed on the other, *If this person is being judgmental towards me, it might be positive judgment now, but at another time it might be a negative judgement.* People also feel very uncomfortable when the judgement of others does not match their view of themselves. The way to appreciate others in the no-problem area through appreciation is to use *I-messages*, rather than *You-messages*.

HELPING

In the helping quadrant, our task is to help others solve their own problems. We do this by using active listening (Gordon, 2000). Most people try to help others by providing a solution and telling the other person what to do. Our efforts in assistance usually start with *'what you should do is...'*, when really most people just want to be listened to, so they can 'sound off' and then work out the solution on their own. After all, we are the best at solving our own problems.

Active listening has four key steps. The first one is whole-of-body listening. You actually have to stop, listen and give the other person signs that you are listening— through either body language or acknowledgements, for example, *I can hear you.* The second step is to listen for facts and feelings. Listening for the emotions or feelings behind the communication is the critical element of active listening. The third step is to reflect to the other person your understanding of the facts and the feelings. Finally, we do that with empathy and acceptance. We may not necessarily feel empathetic or accepting towards our child or our direct report all the time. This is okay, and normal. After all, we are human. However, you cannot use active listening if you are not feeling empathetic and accepting towards the other person. If you try to use this skill when you're not feeling empathetic or accepting, the other person will be left feeling manipulated.

Let's try some examples: when your colleague comes into your office complaining about the IT system and how they still haven't had their laptop properly configured, you can say, *It sounds like you're really frustrated that your laptop's still not operational.* When your boss comes into your office looking downcast because they just can't get the data they need from another department to complete a report, an active listening response would be, *It seems to me that you're really downcast and frustrated about your inability to complete this report on time to keep your boss happy.*

When your child comes home pale from school with their shoulders slumped, you can say, *It looks to me like you've had a rough day today.* When they start complaining about their teacher, you can say, *It sounds like you're really frustrated that your teacher's not listening to you in class.* If your child is playing Lego and you can hear them getting angry and frustrated, you can say, *I can hear that you're really upset that you just can't get your Lego working the way you want it to.*

Here is an example of a longer active listening conversation.

Karen : Do you have a few minutes to give me some help on a problem, Nicole?

Nicole : Sure, Karen, I have half an hour before a meeting, does that work?

Karen: That would be great; it's Sarah, she is starting to drive me mad.

Nicole: Sarah is driving you mad?

Karen: Yeah, I have never known anyone quite like her. Hmm ... she is smart, no question about that. The trouble is she thinks that she knows everything, and every time I suggest something, she finds some reason why it won't work.

Nicole: It's frustrating when she won't listen to your suggestions?

Karen: Yeah, the negativity really frustrates me. I'm her boss and I'm really trying to help her, but she is making it impossible for me to help.

Nicole: So you really don't like the negativity.

Karen: No, I don't. It starts to make me negative and I try very hard to be positive about the introduction of SAP, but I'm finding it hard to deal with, too.

Nicole: So, you are trying hard to be positive about SAP, and the attitude of others is making it difficult?

Karen: Yeah. SAP is annoying, but I'm much more frustrated about dealing with Sarah. You know what? Her constant complaints about how we do things around here makes me feel like the last two years of hard work I have put in here count for nothing. I feel so unappreciated and deflated.

Nicole: You're really feeling quite deflated and demoralised about the progress you have been making in the role.

Karen: Yes, I am … anyway, I guess we have made progress compared to how bad it was last Christmas, so I guess I just need to remember that. It is just hard when others come along and complain. It feels like Sarah is constantly complaining and criticising, which is really annoying. But I guess that she is really trying to do her best and prove herself in the role. I just wish she would stop complaining.

Nicole: So, you think you have made progress with SAP and that Sarah is probably feeling a bit insecure being new to the role?

Karen: Yes, I guess so. I guess I should be a bit less defensive. I have tried not to be defensive, but I guess I can't help myself sometimes. I might go and have a chat to her and apologise for being defensive. I could renew our 'good ideas' register. I set this up six months ago, to deal with an overload of improvement opportunities that came from the SAP implementation. I haven't looked at it for a few months. Perhaps we could revisit in our next team meeting. Then I have a way of channelling her suggestions, which feel are a bit overwhelming right now.

Nicole: So you think you could sort this out with a conversation with Sarah, and revisiting the register? That might help with your overwhelm.

Karen: Yes. I think so. Oh well, back to it, I guess. Thanks for helping out and listening.

A great way to begin active listening is to use a lead-in to your sentence. For example, *It sounds like ... I can hear ... It seems like ... I'm wondering ...* These lead-ins are not essential for active listening, but they help us to begin listening in a way that points us in the right direction.

There are multiple benefits to using active listening skill. It helps the other person solve their problem. As you listen to them, and reflect what you are hearing, it helps them think through and develop a deeper understanding of their problem. As they are listened to, it helps them get to the core of their problem. Often, the presenting problem is really the outer layers of the onion, and as you listen you get closer and closer to the core issue. **When we actively listen to somebody, they have the experience of being listened to.** This is a very powerful experience, and greatly appreciated by them and it strengthens our relationships.

I feel that in our society, very few people have been listened to at all. In fact, I think one of the reasons we have so many counsellors and psychologists is because we are not being listened to—we actually have to pay someone to listen to us!

Being listened to is incredibly therapeutic. It helps us unpack our baggage, our problems, think them through, resolve them and move on. In fact, active listening is a skill used by counsellors and psychologists to help their clients. This has psychological benefits at work and at home. It is wonderful for supporting your children because you become the person that can counsel your child through the challenges of growing up. You become the person that your child comes to for help in resolving their problems. While you are there for your child, during their growing up, you can help them process all their challenges so they don't take a backpack full of problems and baggage into their teenage years and beyond.

Although others say there are no silver bullets to most problems, I believe that active listening can make a dramatic difference to most relationships. If everybody learnt to actively listen, we could change the world.

CONFRONT

Next, we have the **confront** quadrant when you need to communicate with someone whose behaviour is causing you or others a problem. Here, we use an *I-Message*. It is the same skill used when giving performance feedback to your staff. In the work environment, managers must give feedback to their staff, but most managers hate it and avoid it at all costs. They hate giving feedback that might be perceived as negative. They are afraid of anger. They are afraid of upsetting the other person.

The main problem with how most people deliver feedback is that we do it in a very judgmental way by using the pronoun *you*. For example, 'you messed up that project'*; 'you were rude to that client'*. People hate to be judged and they particularly hate to be criticised. Many people will become defensive when criticised and will not hear what you are trying to say. The alternative to the *You-message* is the *I-message*.

There are three key parts to an I-message. The first part is an *accurate* description of the other's behaviour rather than a judgement of them. For example, describing someone as messy is not an accurate description of behaviour. Being *messy* is our value judgment associated with their behaviour of leaving Lego on the floor. Being *irresponsible* **is not** an accurate description of behaviour. Entering a hazardous workplace without appropriate safety equipment and safety clothing **is** an accurate description of behaviour.

Second, there must be a description of the impact of the other person's behaviour on ourselves. For example,

1. (*When you failed to get me that report on time), it meant I had to spend my weekend working on it, when I would have much preferred to have been with my family.*

2. Or at home, (*when you didn't unpack the dishwasher when I asked you to), it meant that I had to do it in a rush this morning, and it made me late for work. Or* (w*hen you wake me in the middle of the night), I'm tired the next morning, and it means I struggle at work all day through tiredness.*

In this part of the I-message, it's essential to describe the impact of the other's behaviour on **us**, not on **them**. Most people (yes, including our children!) are programmed to actually care and to want to help someone else, so a description of the impact of their behaviour on *us* is usually very effective. It's also important that these descriptions of behaviour on us are concrete and tangible, for example, it could cost us time, money, get us in trouble from our boss, or stop us from getting our needs met.

The third part of an I-message, one that makes it particularly powerful, is how it makes us feel—the emotional element. For example,

1. *(When I had to explain to my manager that you had demonstrated unsafe behaviour in front your whole team), I was so embarrassed.*

2. Or at home, *(when you refused to help me clean the table up after dinner, it takes a lot of my time), and I feel really hurt.*

One way of learning and practising I-messages is by using a table below.

Behaviour	Impact on you	Feeling/emotion
Failed to provide report on time	Had to work on weekend to get it to my boss	Annoyed
Don't put on your shoes when I ask	We will be late for kinder and I will be late for work	Worried I will get into trouble from my boss
Don't give your staff any flexibility	We are at risk of losing good staff and impacting team performance	Upset and worried about how to the work done

'When you failed to provide me the report on time, I had to work on the weekend to get it to my boss and I was very annoyed'.

'When you don't put your shoes on when I ask, we will be late for kinder and I will be late for work and I'm worried I will get into trouble from my boss.'

'When you don't provide flexibility for your staff, we are at risk of losing good staff and impacting team performance and I'm upset about this and worried as to how we will get the work done'

I-messages work because they are authentic and less likely to elicit a defensive response. But they don't work all the time. There are two key reasons why I-messages might not work. One is that no matter how much we dislike the behaviour, we may struggle to find the real, concrete, and tangible impact of the behaviour on us so the other person feels no need to change their behaviour. This more often occurs in the parent-child relationship, where we have strong views as to how our children should behave. We call these conflicts of values.

Second, I-messages might not work if the other person has a strong need that is not being met. When we identify that the other person has a strong need, we are actually in the bottom left quadrant and need to use problem solving.

I-messages are particularly useful tools when addressing problems that are causing a negative impact on us, where, if not addressed, they will impact our relationship with the other person. Many people avoid addressing problems they experience with other people. They put up with it, and over time build resentment. This also prevents us providing valuable feedback on performance and how their behaviour is affecting colleagues.

If we do get a negative response from our I-message, we can use *active listening* to help the receiver deal with their emotions and upset. This double combination I-message and the ability to actively listen to others' emotions gives us significant confidence in being able to dramatically improve our relationships with other people.

PROBLEM-SOLVE

In the bottom-left quadrant of the communication square, our goal is to solve both of our problems and get both sets of needs met using the **problem-solving** tool. This is where we draw on our active listening skills to help understand the other party's problem and move into problem solving, and use our I-message to communicate our problem.

STEP 1 is to understand the needs of both parties. We use active listening to understand the other party's needs, and we use I-messages to communicate our needs. This is critical to problem solving. Many people talk about their wants, for example, a husband wants to buy a boat and his wife does not want her husband to buy a boat. It seems that those solutions are not at all compatible. Let's understand the needs that might sit beneath each of needs proposed by each party. Why might the husband want to purchase a boat? There are a range of possible needs: maybe he wants to get away into the outdoors, maybe he wants to escape the rat-race of life, maybe he wants some peace and quiet from his family, maybe he wants to take the kids fishing, or maybe he just wants to show off to his mates. Why might his wife *not* want him to have a boat? Maybe she's concerned about their financial security, maybe she doesn't want a boat clogging up the back garden, maybe she's afraid her husband won't be around to help her look after the kids, or maybe she's afraid that he will take the kids fishing and she's fearful for their safety. Each party has a different set of needs.

STEP 2 is to brainstorm options that get both sets of needs met. The rules of brainstorming are that there are no dumb ideas and you just keep collecting new ideas until the end of the brainstorming session. There are no evaluations of the merits of each idea. The key benefits of this brainstorming methodology are that it opens up creativity. If we don't adopt a brainstorming methodology, with on-the-go evaluations we risk people not making further contributions for fear of ridicule. Once children are over the age of four, I find that they can come up with amazing, creative ideas for getting their problems solved. They're usually more creative than adult ideas. In the workplace, a brainstorming session can generate creativity from different backgrounds.

STEP 3 is to evaluate the options identified in step 2 against the needs that were identified in step 1. For the simple problems, and for problems at home, it's easy to say, *Which of these ideas do we like, so we can choose the best one.* In the workplace, and for more complex problems, we might want to evaluate each of our options more comprehensively.

STEP 4 is deciding what solution we're going to implement.

In the team leadership section of this book, I'll be expanding on problem-solving with our whole team/

SPEAKING SKILLS

The ability to speak to a group larger than one person in a formal setting is a vital ingredient in your leadership and in your personal and professional life. It's worthwhile getting on top of this skill, sooner rather than later. Often people fear standing in front of a group more than they fear death. Speaking in front of groups is like anything else, the more we do it the better we become at the task. It's imperative to start practising this skill early in your career. Learning to speak in front of groups not only accelerates your career, it gives you leverage. I believe that everyone is born with something to deliver and something to share. The way to do that is through public speaking. The key to successful and confident public speaking is to know what you're talking about. Know the intellectual property you are sharing, research it and develop it—become the expert.

DEALING WITH FEAR

A fear of public speaking puts a handbrake on your career and your enjoyment of life. There are books, blogs, and articles on how to deal with fear of public speaking. Being the expert is a great start, but there are other relevant techniques.

First, remember that your public speaking serves others. It has nothing to do with you. And those attending your talks are there for themselves, not for you. Eighty per cent of the thoughts we have each day are of ourselves. People want to hear your talk to benefit themselves. Keep an attitude of service.

Breathing, meditative, and visualisation techniques can be useful in helping calm your nerves. Natalie Brewer runs a business called Heart Speakers. She uses a range of yogic processes to help embed our key messages into our heart. I find these processes incredibly helpful when connecting to my message, and coming across authentically. Of course, the final method of overcoming fears is, to quote the footwear giant, Nike—just do it. Sometimes, we just have to do something. As we conquer our fears, we increase our circle of comfort; we increase our effectiveness; and most importantly, we increase our enjoyment of life. There are plenty of ways to practice public speaking. Start by joining Toastmasters or other speaking groups. These groups offer you accelerated opportunities to stand up in front of other people.

BEING AN EXPERT

Becoming the expert is the key to *quality* public speaking. Most of us see this as a mysterious process that must take a lifetime and only happens to others. In fact, like many things, there is a recipe to becoming an expert, and it's a lot easier than you think.

The first step is to research your topic. If you read the key material around a particular topic, you will be an expert compared to everybody else that you're working with, so read classic and current texts, and subscribe to a blog on your chosen topic.

Next you need a system to be able to develop and record your intellectual property. For this purpose, I recommend *Sell Your Thoughts* by Matt Church and Peter Cook. This book outlines the process for capturing your thoughts and developing them. This process not only documents your thoughts, it provides a way of collecting data to back up your thought-leadership. This data is either left-brain or rational: data, facts, statistics, case studies; or right brain: stories and experiences.

It is also essential to develop metaphors for communicating your intellectual property. Metaphors and stories are incredibly powerful ways to communicate your thoughts and ideas to others. To become a good public speaker, as an expert in your field, you must know your intellectual property and the point you want to share. You must then share that point in a multitude of different ways supported by rational and social data, and with powerful metaphors and stories.

When you're an expert on something you care about or are interested in, speaking to others about it becomes joyous and easy. Your knowledge (or expertise) on a topic affords you confidence to relax and enjoy the process.

MANAGERIAL SKILLS

ONE-ON-ONE MANAGERIAL RELATIONSHIPS

Managing other people is a great opportunity to contribute more to an organisation. I deliberately use the word 'manager' rather than 'leader' in this context. Anyone can be a leader in a multitude of different ways and in different contexts. A 'manager' is a 'manager' by virtue of being appointed by an organisation into a role that is accountable for leading other people as part of the organisational structure. One of the accountabilities of a manager is to lead their team. Hence, a manager needs leadership skills.

A manager in an organisation has particular accountabilities and is required to undertake specific tasks. Unfortunately, the training we provide to most managers is inadequate. We spend years getting our undergraduate degree, mostly for technical elements to our profession, and we study maths, physics, and dynamics, yet we don't study how to lead other people. Even those who study business or hold a Masters of Business Administration are poorly equipped to lead other people. Being a manager of another person is an incredibly powerful and privileged position. Abuse of that power can lead to poor outcomes for employees who are stressed and humiliated, and are set up to fail. While most of us can tell a story about a bad boss, few of us are willing to recognise that sometimes we are the bad boss.

There are critical things a manager must do to build trust and be effective in their role. In this section, I will be describing the key accountabilities and knowledge that a manager must have in order to effectively lead other people. The role of a manager is critical because it is the key or translating the purpose of the organisation to the workers at the frontline, whose job it is to implement the tasks that the organisation need completed. In its most basic state, an organisation is a group of people who have gathered to deliver against a purpose. The task is too big for one person, so multiple people must coordinate their efforts, and work together to deliver the purpose. Organisations are social units held together by the formal and informal relationships between individuals in the organisation.

The effectiveness of the organisation to deliver against its purpose is a function of how well those people can coordinate their activities. The coordination of these activities is dependent on the organisational infrastructure that has been constructed to enable the organisation to do its work. By organisation infrastructure, I mean the organisational structure, the clear articulation of accountabilities of each team member within that structure and the organisation's systems and processes that enable the work to be completed. Within this organisational infrastructure, managers effectively drive the organisation through appropriate managerial practices. That is, the things managers do to enable the work to get done.

The rest of this section describes the managerial practices that good managers undertake to get the necessary work done. I like to think of organisations as being like a tree with many branches. At each of the nodes between the main branch and the sub-branch is the manager, and the viability and the health of the sub-branch is dependent on the performance of the manager. Managerial performance is critical to organisational effectiveness.

From the employees' perspective, the quality and the performance of their manager is critical to their own performance, and their own emotional and psychological well-being. Every individual is motivated to do their best in their role. Employees will do their best despite the manager, and despite their organisation. Bad management, for an employee, can be extraordinarily stressful and can take a real toll on the employee's emotional and mental health. There are huge opportunities for productivity improvement in Australia's organisations through improving managerial effectiveness.

When I was 40, and returning from maternity leave, I was appointed General Manager of Customer Operations at Yarra Valley Water. Previously, I had been the General Manager of Marketing and Strategy, and in that role I'd managed more than 30 highly-professional and capable people. But now, I was daunted by managing a team of 150 people, which included the Customer Contact Centre of 80 people.

Despite the fact that I had an MBA under my belt, it's fair to say that I really did not know what I was supposed to actually do from day to day, as a General Manager. It is easy for a manager to be busy by dipping into the work of those who report to them, but this is not very effective and can undermine their direct reports. I remember sitting in a meeting room with Sheila Deane, whom I trusted, and confessed my fears and anxiety that I really did not know what to do. Sheila helped me understand my actual role as a General Manager from a daily perspective. Thanks to Sheila, I developed into a highly competent and effective manager of people. I dedicate the rest of this chapter to Sheila, for explaining to me the key role of managers. Her work is drawn from Elliott Jaques's life work as a researcher, who spent his entire career studying organisations. He is known for developing the body of work known as Requisite Organisation.

In the next chapters, I'll include a summary of the key roles of a manager. For those who wish to delve deeper into this work, I refer you to *Leading People* by Peter Mills, which summarises the work of Sheila and Barry Dean, or *Requisite Organization*, by Elliott Jaques.

TRUST

Trust is an essential element in effective organisations. Organisations are groups of people working together to achieve a common purpose. They are inherently social units. The key to successful and productive social interactions is trust. For an organisation to be effective, there must be trust between all employees, but most critically, there must be trust between a manager and a direct report. A direct report must trust a manager will fulfil their commitments, treat them fairly and with consideration, and trust their judgment.

Trust is a bit like oxygen to the organisation: without it, the organisation will suffocate and die. An organisation with low levels of trust is a toxic organisation. They are toxic to the performance of the organisation and to the mental health and well-being of its employees. Low levels of trust lead people to seek guidance from unions or other representatives who can help them maintain a sense of control. However, interference from a union or human resources department may further undermine trust levels between the manager and employee.

In the early 1980s, Sir Roderick Carnegie was the chairperson of CRA (now Rio Tinto) that owned Hamersley Iron. Hamersley Iron was struggling. It was unable to reliably ship iron ore to the Japanese steel mills because the mines were routinely disrupted with extended periods of industrial action. There was a continuing battle between the employees and management at the mine, for control of resources and conditions for the employee. There were low levels of trust.

Carnegie realised that the cause of the strong union power was due to low levels of trust between employees and their managers and within the organisation as a whole. He hired Professor Elliott Jaques to help develop a comprehensive and disciplined approach to organisational leadership, with the prime goal of improving trust between manager and employee. The outcomes dramatically improved the efficiency and effectiveness of the Hamersley Iron operations, which had benefits for both the business and the employees. After all, it is in both the employees' and the organisation's best interest that the organisation be efficient and effective at delivering its purpose.

'Trust between people is the basic social glue. Suspicion and mistrust are the prime enemies of reasonable human relationships.'—Elliot Jaques

It is the role of a manager to build quality relationships and high levels of trust with their employees. Every manager must consider the following before making a decision: will my action(s) induce or undermine trust? Trust and relationships are enhanced through open, authentic, and honest communication. Yes, there are times when a manager cannot confide information to an employee. Again, this should be addressed openly and honestly. If you are asked for information you cannot divulge, explain that, *No, unfortunately I cannot share that information with you now*. Explain the reason for it, and make a commitment to that employee that you will share the information as soon as you're able and as soon as it becomes available.

Remember that trust is built slowly. Simon Sinek says, that you cannot immediately understand the impact of a decision that you make in terms of building your trust and your leadership. It's a bit like going to the gym once, coming home, looking in the mirror and feeling disappointment as not seeing a difference.

However, after three month's dedication you will notice a difference.

Do not underestimate the impact of trust on your direct report's psychological and emotional well-being. Employees will be loyal to a manger whom they trust and an organisation that shares their purpose and values. Employees are inherently motivated to do their best, and everybody wants to do meaningful work.

ACCOUNTABILITY

Being accountable means that you can be 'called to account' for the delivery of the tasks you have been allocated. It also means that you have the authority to give account. Accountability is different from responsibility. Responsibility is an internally generated feeling of concern around the outcomes. I might feel responsible for ensuring that the children at my child's birthday party have a good time, but in my work, I am held accountable for ensuring the effective and efficient operation of a contact centre whose job is to answer queries from customers. This accountability for the contact centre has been bestowed on me by the organisation, and the organisation will hold me to account for its performance.

As managers, we have several accountabilities. We're accountable for:

- our own personal effectiveness.

- the output of the entire team.

- building a team that is capable of delivering the required work.

- leading that team, which requires getting the willing commitment of all team members to work together in the direction set by the manager.

- leading change and continuous improvement within the team.

AUTHORITIES

To be effective in our role as manager, we need *authorities* that match our *accountabilities,* particularly if we are to be held accountable for the output of our team. One of the greatest problems in corporate Australia is the number of roles where accountability and authority are not matched. Giving people accountability to deliver something, but where they don't have the authority to control delivery, is grossly unfair and unreasonable, and puts the individual under considerable stress.

People in these roles are reduced to finding ways to influence others (which could include bribing or bullying). all of which are unproductive activities, and draining and dispiriting for the individual. In an accountable organisation, it's not okay to say, *We couldn't deliver against this assignment because Joe, over here, is useless.* If we are accountable for the performance of our team, we must have the authority to enable us to deliver against these accountabilities.

As managers, need the following authorities:

- power of veto over the appointment of people to our team. We cannot be expected to be accountable for delivery if we're given team members who are not capable of delivering the work. The power of veto means we can review the inclusion of a team member by giving reasonable explanation as to why that person cannot deliver in the role

- exclusive authority to assign tasks to their team members.

- to review and provide feedback, and to reward and recognise the work performed by the team.

- initiate the removal of an individual from a role if that person cannot deliver against the tasks required. Managers do not have the right to dismiss an individual from their team. They must approach their manager and explain the situation. It is their manager's job to work out the next steps to ensure the team has right capabilities and that the individuals are treated with respect and dignity—essential for organisational trust.

WHAT EVERY EMPLOYEE NEEDS TO KNOW

Every employee has the right to know the answer to the following four questions. Each manager must answer these questions for each of their direct reports.

1. *As an organisation, where are we going?* All employees must know the purpose of an organisation. What is the organisation trying to achieve? It is the manager's role to interpret the organisation's overall purpose and goal to the purpose and goal their team.

2. *What is my role?* A manager must be able to describe their direct report's role in delivering against the organisation's goals and purpose. The manager must make each direct report aware of what they are accountable for delivering.

3. *How am I performing? How am I going in my role?* A manager must give clear feedback as to what's going well, and what's not going well.

4. *What is my future in this organisation?* Am I suitable to other roles within the company? This question needs to be answered by your manager's manager. We call this person the manager once removed.

It is the fundamental human right of every employee to know the answers to the above four question.

TASK ASSIGNMENT

A manager is accountable for assigning tasks to their direct reports. Task assignment is generally poorly done in Australian corporations. A proper task assignment needs to achieve a specific output within a given period and within given resources. Often staff are allocated unclear or ambiguous tasks, at which they work at hard to deliver only for the manager to be disappointed because the results are unexpected. Unclear allocation of tasks is extremely wasteful of company resources, as time and effort is put into an activity that was not required because it was poorly specified. This is also soul-destroying to the employee who worked hard to deliver the task.

The chronic cynicism that exists in many corporations today is a result of so many people spending time delivering against activities that make no real contribution. Everyone is inherently motivated to make a difference. Everyone wants to do a good job and deliver the best they can, but when managers aren't capable of clearly articulating what they need, motivation and goodwill is squandered.

As a manager, you're authorised to allocate tasks *to your direct reports only*. You're not authorised to allocate tasks to another manager's direct report. This practice of inappropriate task allocation damages and undermines the relationship between a direct report and his or her manager. When you allocate a task to your direct report, then it is their job to allocate any sub-tasks to those who report to them.

When a manager dips too far down and assigns tasks to the direct report of their direct report, it makes it very difficult for the manger in the middle to get the required work done. Clearly, this is a considerable waste of company resources, but more importantly, it diminishes the limited amount of goodwill and enthusiasm of your staff members and undermines the essential trust between a manager and an employee.

Effective task assignment requires addressing the key elements of Context, Purpose, Quantity, Quality, Resources and Time (CPQQRT). Assigning tasks is a social process. It needs to be done in consultation with the people who are going to complete the task. This can be one-on-one with a direct report or with a team by using the team-working process (see section on leading teams), depending on the scope and impact of the task. All task assignments, except for the simplest, need to be documented for clarity and to enable referral back to the original task as the task proceeds.

Context is critical for the assignment of tasks. People are far more engaged and likely to deliver a better output if they understand the context of the task. The context includes how this task fits into the overall purpose and business plan of the organisation. and how it fits into other activities within the organisation. When the task is to solve long-standing issues, the history as to why we need this task can be very useful. When documenting the task assignment, the section on context could be quite lengthy and you may need to refer to other documents or sources.

Identifying the **purpose** of the task is essential and should be distilled into one sentence. Examples of this could be providing water to a new suburb, making recommendations on the best piece of software to use for storing customer data or a device to improve hearing.

Quantity describes how *many* of *what* the output is. For example, one pumping station, one report, or 50,000 widgets.

Quality is the description of the output required. The quality includes all the specifications with which the output must comply. If we're building a pumping station, the quality section would include the amount of water to be pumped, elevations, types of pump to be considered, descriptions of the pumping station, noise requirements and budgets.

The example of making a recommendation on the best computing system could be lengthy. This section could include detailed and full business requirements of the new computer system.

The **resource** section includes a description of all resources available to complete the task. It will include the budget, equipment and estimated hours for people. **Timing** is the task deadline. and may also include project milestone dates.

When I started in a new role as General Manager of Customer Operations at Yarra Valley Water, half my day consisted of people coming into my office with concerns about activities that others were doing, *Jenny, did you know that so-and-so is doing a project over here that's going to cause me a problem. It will mean I won't get what I need to be able to deliver to my customers.* I felt like I was constantly firefighting. Consequently, my team sat down and identified issues and options, and documented the task assignment taking input from each team member in a social process. I came away from that process with several pages of copied whiteboard notes and spent another couple of hours documenting a task assignment. I felt like I was taking an inordinate amount of time meeting with my team and documenting this task.

I allocated the tasks to the relevant people, all of whom had the full context because of the team-working process. In a regular one-on-one meeting a couple of weeks later, I asked a team member how project implementation was proceeding. I was amazed to hear that that task had been completed with no implementation issues. I realised that implementation was made easy by involving everyone from the beginning and providing clear task assignment. The process of documenting the task assignment added enormous value to everyone, and it provided absolute clarity and ensured the implementation of the correct solutions.

FIT FOR ROLE

One of the accountabilities of a manager is to develop a capable team able to deliver the work that is required. To develop a capable team, not only do we need to know and understand what roles are required in the team, we need to hire capable and competent people to fill those roles. Very often, we become a manager of an existing team. In this case, it's essential to check that the team has the capability to deliver the work required. There are three key elements in ensuring that you have capable people to fill the right roles in your team. The first is: does this individual have the knowledge, skills and experience to complete the required work? Sometimes you might have a candidate or a role incumbent that does not fully have the knowledge, skills and experience for the role. However, each of these can be developed by providing opportunities for that individual to gain necessary knowledge, develop necessary skills, and undertake projects that will deliver them the necessary experience. The second key element is: does the individual have values and preferences for work that match those of the role? That is, are they going to enjoy the work? Do they like the work? Do they value it? We all have different value sets and temperaments, which make different roles of interest or not. Whether we value our work (or not) is an innate attribute of the individual. For example, although I think it's important to generate financial reports, I'm completely uninterested in preparing them myself. I'm not good at detail and accuracy; I like to think of the big picture. These are attributes which would make being in a financial reporting role extremely difficult and frustrating for me, and I would likely fail. No amount of coercion, encouragement, practice or effort is going to make me good at being a financial reporter.

Finally, a candidate or incumbent must have the intellectual capacity to deal with the complexity of the role. We call it the work-ability of the role. Roles inside organisations, depending on how far up or down the structure they are, have different role requirements for the ability to deal with complexity. Think 'applied IQ'. For example, the role of running an organisation at CEO level requires a higher level of aptitude to deal with complexity and intellectual capability than that of driving a bus. It also requires us to plan or see much farther into the future. It is essential that we match the roles to the capabilities. If we put someone with a higher level of capability into a role that does not require that capability, that individual will quickly get bored and frustrated. If we put an individual that does not have the intellectual capability for the role they're required to perform, they will become stressed and overwhelmed. They will start micromanaging their direct reports because they will feel much more comfortable at doing that level of work.

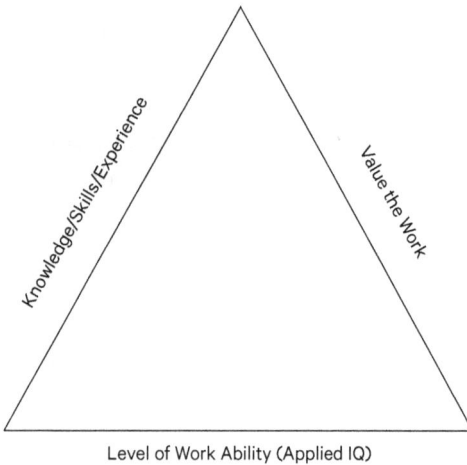

Level of Work Ability (Applied IQ)

Again, we cannot change people's intellectual capabilities, although these capabilities do grow and mature over time as a person develops. Getting the right people into the right roles is a bit like completing a jigsaw puzzle. No matter how much we would like a particular piece to fit, if it is the wrong piece, it is the wrong piece. And no matter how hard we try as managers, sometimes people are not going to be an appropriate fit for their role.

The best thing we can do with individuals we deem unsuitable to a role is to fit them with an appropriate one. Placing blame, and dismissing them as useless, is far too prevalent in corporate Australia today. It is extremely damaging to individuals. If you are not enjoying your role, it's not necessarily your fault. Maybe you're a poor fit for the role or maybe the role is poorly designed. Rather than putting all your energy into the current role, you might be better advised to find a new role more suited to your knowledge, skills and experience, values and preferences, and intellectual capability.

PROVIDING FEEDBACK

Providing feedback to direct reports on their performance is something most managers find extraordinarily difficult. As a result, many people never receive feedback and either continue to perform poorly or develop high levels of anxiety. They know something isn't right, but no one ever actually helps by providing constructive feedback.

Giving feedback to others is difficult because no one, except the odd psychopath, really wants to hurt other people's feelings. We're afraid of the other person's strong emotions—upsetting feelings, or anger. I've heard many a grown man say, *I can deal with anything that's thrown at me, but not tears*. Seeing other people upset makes us upset, and we feel their emotional pain. Seeing other people angry is just plain scary.

The assertiveness skill described in the chapter on relationships enables us to give feedback in a far less offensive manner, and in a way that is less likely to elicit a defensive response. When we use an I-message (when you ... the impact on me is ... and that makes me feel ...) we are less judgemental than a 'You-message' and people don't like to be judged. Additionally, with active listening skills under your belt, if they are upset you can help them move through it and help them resolve their upset.

Giving quality feedback is one of the greatest gifts you can offer, and when it is done with skill, honesty and compassion, it can be extremely powerful. Feedback is not something you provide during that horrible performance management discussion that HR dictates you must have every six months (or annually); it is something that you can, and should, provide to your direct report in 'real time', whenever a piece of work is delivered, and at your weekly one-on-one meetings.

You can open a feedback conversation with, *How did you go with this piece of work? What could have been done differently to make this piece of work easier? What have you learned from this piece of work?* With questions like these, your employee will most likely answer all of them, and deliver their feedback to themselves. Most people are not stupid, and they know what went well and what didn't.

The key is not to be afraid of feedback, but to develop the skills to deliver feedback respectfully and with compassion. Then you know you're giving a beautiful gift that will help strengthen your relationship and help them improve their performance.

MEET WITH YOUR DIRECT REPORTS

A weekly one-on-one session with each of your direct reports is critical. It's like the floor in your relationship building. Quality relationships are developed when we spend one-on-one time with the other person. If you don't hold these meetings, problems will remain unsolved, and you will be interrupted or ambushed later. If a direct report knows they have the opportunity to talk with a manager one-on-one, and on a regular basis, they will confidently gather all their issues and deal with them simultaneously. If you regularly cancel these meetings, you are sending them the message that they are not valued. This undermines performance, trust and loyalty.

Here is a sample agenda for a one-on-one meeting with your direct report.

1. Check in to see how they are going. Build rapport and trust. Spend five minutes asking, *How was your day? How are things going at work?* Over time, as your relationship strengthens, find opportunities to talk about children, families, and hobbies. The quality of these relationships is important to the health of the organisation. The amount of empathy you demonstrate will reflect in their level of comfort and trust enabling them to have open, honest discussions, engender loyalty to you and the

organisation, and enhance employee engagement and performance.

2. What issues or challenges are they currently facing at work? Often people need help in getting their tasks done. They need either advice or assistance in navigating the organisation or team. As a manager, you will have insight into their challenges and the solution by virtue of your capability, position and authority.

3. Use the problem-solving methodology to help resolve the challenges and issues of your direct report is experiencing.

4. This is your opportunity to assign new tasks. Share a documented (draft) task assignment. Take your direct report through this task and ask for their feedback, comments, and thoughts and incorporate these into the task assignment as appropriate.

5. Monitor the tasks already in place and address any relevant Key Performance Indicators (KPIs). This is your chance to discover how a particular project is going. Remember that you're accountable for the output, so use this opportunity to gain knowledge of a project's progress and assess and manage risks of project failure.

6. Provide performance feedback.

7. Seek feedback from them on your own or company performance.

Running quality, one-on-one meetings with your direct reports will dramatically improve your team leadership.

TEAM LEADERSHIP SKILLS

MANAGERIAL ONE-TO-MANY

The previous section described the skills you need to interact successfully with each of your direct reports. This section describes the skills required to successfully operate your team as a group.

TEAM PURPOSE

Managers must know the direction their company is taking. They must understand the purpose of the company, why it exists, who its customers are, and what its vision and goals are. Although this sounds self-evident, it is surprising how few people, lower down in the company ladder, truly understand the company's goals. Not only must a manager understand the goals and objectives of the company, they must be able to interpret them for their team.

Having purpose is a critical human need, and aligning the purpose of an individual with that of the organisation's goals is not only incredibly powerful and useful for the organisation, it also provides meaning and value to an individual's life. The role of a manager, at each level in the organisation, is to understand the company's objectives and interpret that for their team, providing detail appropriate to each level.

It's a bit like catching the train across the country—unless you know your destination, you're unlikely to make the right connections to get to your destination.

'If a manager does not keep his or her immediate subordinates well informed about where the manager is coming from, they are at sea. They will not be able to work with understanding and they are deprived of the joy that comes from understanding from being in the picture.'—Dr Elliott Jaques

Debate and conversation is a critical element of creating meaning and understanding. Don't be afraid to invest time with your team to help them understand the company's direction and what it means for them, your investment will pay off.

PLANNING

A manager must plan the work required of the team. As it's been said before: a failure to plan is planning to fail. A manager must plan the work of their team as well as their own output. Plans should cascade through the organisation. The CEO is accountable, with the support of his or her staff, for developing a business plan for the entire organisation. This business plan is then developed in detail for each team by the manager of each team, with the input of their direct reports.

The accountability for developing a plan for your team cannot be delegated. You must develop the plan, although, other people can assist you in various tasks associated with the plan development. As the leader of your team, only you can develop a plan that describes what all members of the team need to deliver. It is not the purpose of this book to describe and outline processes of business planning, except to note that most business plans are long, wordy, and unclear, meaning that an enormous number of plans are developed and shelved until, at the end of the year, performance reviews are measured against that plan. For those of you running small teams, planning may be as simple as identifying the three critical tasks that need to be completed in the next 12 months, and the steps required to implement those. Of course, plans are best developed in conjunction with your team. Don't be afraid to set aside time, as a group, to share and develop a shared meaning of what your team needs to deliver. This will have significant benefits in building relationships and shared meaning, and dramatically improving the likelihood of actually achieving what you've planned.

TEAM AND ROLE DESIGN

Once the planning is complete, it's essential to ensure that you have the right roles inside your team to be able to deliver the work. It's a bit like conducting an orchestra. The planning phase identifies the pieces of music to be played. Role design describes who plays which piece of music. The conductor tells each of his musicians which parts in the music they need to play. Each manager is accountable for the design of the roles within their team, in consultation with their manager. It's not HR's job to design a role and a position description; however, HR should provide general templates and guidance to ensure consistency of role design across the organisation. Many organisations make the mistake of trying to design roles around the needs and desires of an **individual**. It is essential that roles are designed around the needs and the requirements of the **business** and the work that needs to be done. Then business selects the right people to match those roles. Organising roles around people is often what causes this constant churn and change of business structures, leading to a massive waste of effort and a squandering of goodwill.

Organisational structures have both a horizontal and a vertical element. The vertical elements of a structure or level needs to be dictated by the complexities of the tasks that are required. Many organisations have too many levels and too many managers in their organisation. This again leads to wasted effort, as managers trip over each other and employees have too many levels to negotiate to get important decisions made. Elliot Jaques undertook a detailed study of how many levels an organisation should require, and most organisations in Australia should have a maximum of five levels from top to bottom (but many needs only four).

The horizontal design of a team or organisation should be designed in accordance with the 'value chain': the logical process for getting the work done. For example, Yarra Valley Water engaged three key processes. First, we connected new properties to our water and sewerage network; second, we provided those properties with a water and sewerage services; and third, we billed them for the service. Hence, at a high level we had three General Managers in charge of each of these steps. I was the General Manager of the Billing function and I had managers for the subsets in billing. Step one, read the meter, step two, create and send the bill, step three, answer queries from customers about their bill (Contact Centre), step four, collect the money. In addition to these key process roles, you may have support functions like human resources, process improvement (Six Sigma/ Lean), accounting, property management or strategy, to help those in operational roles.

The best way to start designing roles is to start with what I call a thumbnail. This is a high-level summary of the accountabilities of each member in your team. These accountabilities can be incorporated into a formal position description later. An example of a thumbnail for a start-up engineering business is shown in Appendix B. Once you have developed your draft thumbnail, meet with your team (with the draft document), go through each line item, and confirm accuracy, identify any omissions and update as required. This process is useful for identifying a complete list of accountabilities for your team. Additionally, each team member gets clarity on what they will be held accountable for, and what they can rely on their colleagues to provide to enable them to do their job. This process should be repeated on an annual basis and when there are new team members appointed.

BUILDING TEAM CAPABILITY

You are accountable for the output of your team and for building and leading a team that has the capability of delivering the work required. Leading a team requires your team to *willingly* follow the path described. Your team must not only comprise individuals with the capability to do the work, but they must work cooperatively and collaboratively to achieve the required team output. This is a *social* process. You must set the expectations and conditions for collaboration. Make sure your team understands this, and hold them accountable for delivering their own work and supporting their colleagues to complete their work. The critical prerequisites for providing the conditions for team-work are that your team must meet together and work together. There is little need for artificial 'team-working' exercises like ropes courses for executives. Working teams build team-work and quality relationships by working together to solve problems and achieve outcomes for the team. Below is a description of the 'team-working process' that enables your team to work together to 'get the work done'.

TEAM-WORKING PROCESS

Learning to master the team-working process will take your management from ordinary to outstanding. Organisations are social units, comprising individuals who get together to achieve something they cannot do on their own—the whole is greater than the sum of the parts. The team-working process is what we actually do in order to make this happen. This is how we get our team together: the inputs and the capability of each team member in a coordinated fashion to solve the problems that matter.

Many organisations have problems and opportunities for improvement. Everyone has their own 'solution' to the problem, which seems obvious from their own perspective. Team members engage in 'lobbying' their manager to get what they see as the 'right' decision made. The best lobbyist usually wins and the losers will be upset and consciously or unconsciously sabotage the chosen solution. The team-working process is the antidote to this, and is the method of getting the right solutions.

The team-working process is the essence of team leadership. And if I'm ever asked why I would want to lead a team, or an organisation for that matter, my response is, 'there is no greater joy in life than solving problems that matter, with people you respect and trust'.

The eight-step team-working process is outlined in the diagram below. It is essential that all team members understand that they are accountable for fully contributing to the team-working process. It is not acceptable to not share key information. It is essential that all people who have an interest in the issue and its resolution are in attendance, regardless of their role status and description.

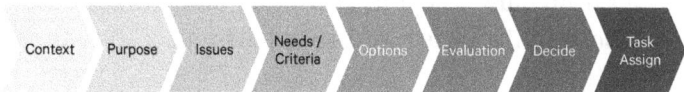

| Context | Purpose | Issues | Needs / Criteria | Options | Evaluation | Decide | Task Assign |

STEP ONE:

Provide the context to the problem. As the team leader, you are accountable for providing the context and inviting your team members to contribute. When people understand the context for the work to be done. it's a bit like adding a fuel additive to the petrol tank. They are able to bring much more to the task because they understand the 'Why'. People do not want to put effort into something they think is a waste of time (even if they are being paid); they want to know why something is important. When you have shared the context, invite the contributions of others. I'm constantly amazed, when I've run these processes, to think that I know the context, only to have someone else provide a critical piece of context to why the problem exists at all, some bit of history as to how this problem occurred, that dramatically improves our understanding of the issues and problems.

STEP TWO:

Write a one-line purpose on a whiteboard. Explain *why* the purpose is relevant, and ask your team to review the purpose, so you can make adjustments. How often are we knee-deep in some project only to ask, *why are we doing this again?* Organisations are full of things that we *could* do, but unless there's a clear purpose for them, they are just distractions and a waste of resources. Once the purpose has been documented on a whiteboard, your team must accept it; and if they don't, rework the purpose until it is clear and accepted by all.

STEP THREE:

Identify all the issues associated with the problem. Everybody gets the opportunity to express their concerns. At this point, you simply document their concerns and refrain from commenting (and certainly from dismissing them), until everybody has spoken. Ask each person to nominate an issue; if they can't think of one they can choose to pass—this will allow consideration for the introverts in the room. You'll probably be left with a whiteboard of stuff that is difficult to assimilate and understand. Sorting these issues into a 'fish-bone' diagram makes it more manageable to grasp of the scope and relevant issues of the problem. If people become upset about a concern, you have an opportunity to use active listening, which will improve understanding of the issue and provide them with the opportunity to express and make sense of their concerns. This will not only help them feel listened to and understood, but will also help you and the rest of the team understand, more deeply, the nature of their concern or anxiety around a particular issue.

STEP FOUR:

Identify the needs of all relevant parties. The relevant parties could include customers, stakeholders, employees, and the organisation. The needs of each party are usually very clear once all of the issues have been identified. Again, active listening can help identify the needs and concerns of the *team*, but you can also use I-messages to communicate *your* needs, or the needs of the *organisation,* which you represent as the manager of the team.

STEP FIVE:

Identify options for solving the problems. This is your traditional brainstorming methodology where you accept all ideas—they're not evaluated at this time.

STEP SIX:

Evaluate the options. A manager's method for evaluating the options will depend on the complexity of the problem, and all options must be evaluated against the needs of all parties. In many brainstorming processes, evaluating the options is as simple as putting a tick, cross, question mark against each of the options. The preferred option will become obvious based on these discussions. For more complex problems, further analysis might be required to collect data, such as costings. Here you would use a different process of weighting each option against each criteria in a matrix. This, for example, is the type of evaluation that will ensure that a piece of software meets the requirements of a business.

STEP SEVEN:

Make a decision. Although this sounds rather obvious, it's amazing how many team leaders and organisations actually avoid making decisions, for fear of getting it wrong or upsetting people. In some organisations, survival is best achieved by making no decisions whatsoever. Unfortunately, that means you'd be part of a low-achieving team. It's the manager's job to decide what option to adopt, and it's the team's job to accept the decision. Once you've taken your team through this entire team-working process, included all the information, content, and ideas, it is highly unlikely that your team would disagree with the decision you've made, particularly if you've clearly articulated why you've made that decision. It is unacceptable for team members to walk out of a team-working process, having neither contributed to nor supported the decision, to then undermine the decision at a later point. Conversations need to continue until direct reports accept the decision.

STEP EIGHT:

Assign tasks. Tasks must be assigned to the relevant people to implement a solution. The team leader must document the tasks and share them clearly, one-on-one, with those who will complete them.

Once this team-working process is complete, your team will have an excellent understanding of the purpose, the issues and why the decisions have been made. This puts you in the box seat, and dramatically improves the likelihood of successful implementation of the agreed solutions.

When I first started using this process, I was anxious that I was spending too much time in meetings. But quality, well-run meetings, like this team-working process, solve problems, and are worthy of the time investment. I found that implementation was easy after taking the time to complete the team-working process. There was no conflict or angst, and a successful outcome was more likely. More importantly, we avoided implementing things that were clearly wrong. The key to success is including everyone in the process so they feel heard, and they understand why decisions are being made, even if the decision may not advantage them personally. I highly recommend becoming a master of this team-working process.

TEAM MEETINGS

Weekly team meetings are essential. Meetings have a bad reputation for being boring and a waste of time. Many poorly-run meetings are exactly this. Team meetings must be led by the leader of the team. The agenda should include:

Check in: How are people going?

Strategy: Communicate any external issues that are relevant to the company. Share any issues of concern and ask for team contributions.

Monitor the progress of tasks that involve more than one team member (in addition to monitoring this task in one-on-one meetings).

Problem solve: Invite team members to bring issues/ challenges to this forum to get advice, support, and feedback to enable the team member to continue their task.

Teamwork: Identify any issues that need to be 'team-worked' across the business. Identify context of issue, the purpose of the task and key individuals that need to be involved in resolving the issue. Either solve problems using the team-working process (if the necessary people are there and you have time) or set a separate meeting to problem solve the individual issue with all the relevant people, regardless of their position in the company.

Monitor: On a monthly basis, review KPIs and identify any relevant issues.

Chapter 5

MINDSET

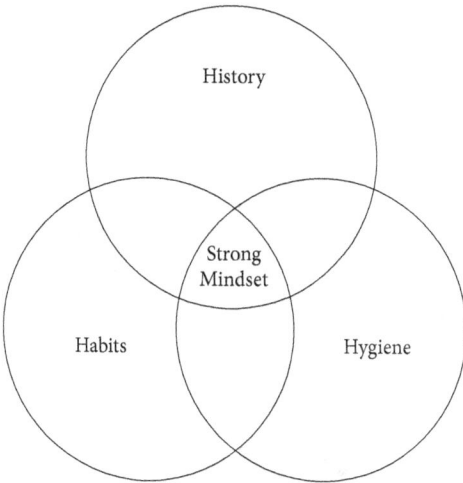

History

Strong
Mindset

Habits

Hygiene

Mindset Model

The third element of our Curating Confidence Model is managing mindset. So much of our lives have been dominated by learning new information or academic or technical skills. Yet arguably, what goes on in our head and our mindset is the most important element to our success and long-term happiness. There are three elements to our mindset: history, hygiene, and habits.

By history, I mean understanding, processing, and letting go of issues, disappointments and traumas that have occurred in our history—from childhood to now. Many childhood experiences prevent a person meeting their full potential. Addressing these issues can have a profound effect on your future. Then there is the hygiene of our thoughts and finally, our habits. What habits can you develop for a successful mindset?

MINDSET BASICS

CURRENT REALITY

beyondblue estimates that 45 per cent of Australians will suffer a mental health issue some time in their lifetime, and that there are 1 million suffers of depression and 2 million suffers of anxiety in Australia at any time. The World Health Organisation (WHO) suggests that mental health issues are one of the leading health problems worldwide. We know so much about our physical bodies yet, as a society, our ability to maintain high levels of mental health seems particularly poor. Even for those who are not suffering anxiety or depression (or other more serious mental health issues) it seems fair to say that the majority of Australians do not have high levels of mental wellness to enable them to be truly high performing. The majority of people are not achieving to their full potential because of limitations of their mindset. It is like our whole country is stuck in second gear and are not driving at top speed.

BRAIN BASICS

Understanding the basics of how our brains work is helpful for maintaining a positive mindset, managing our emotions and avoiding mental health problems. The brain contains over 100 billion neurons and is incredibility complex. As a society, we are only really starting to understand the brain and the mind, and how they work. In fact, it is only in recent decades that people have begun to understand and believe the concept of the brain/body connection. In Chapter 4, we talked about the basic brain design comprising the reptilian (instinctual), mammalian (emotional) and primate (rational) parts of our brain and how, when the emotions are highly aroused. the rational part of the brain is bypassed and we respond from instinct.

We all have a set of beliefs and values that form who we are. The beliefs and patterns define how we respond to any given situation. For example, if we believe that a child having a tantrum is trying to manipulate us then we will 'disapprove of the tantrum' and find ways to make the child stop. If we believe that punishment is the best way of controlling a child's behaviour, then we will punish the child. If we believe that a tantrum means the child is upset and the best way to deal with a tantrum is to listen to them, then we will listen to them. Our belief systems define our behaviour.

These belief systems and value sets are unique to each of us, and are established through our childhood and life experiences. Much of our belief systems are passed down to us from our parents. Other defining beliefs are decisions that we make based on our childhood experiences.

All of us, at some stage, made a decision as a result of a childhood experience that:

- there is something wrong with us.

- that we don't belong.

- that we are on our own.

Everyone suffers from some version of these belief systems. I call them different flavours—like everyone has an ice-cream cone but everyone is eating a different flavour. These belief systems then define our behaviour patterns. My own version looks like this: I am only loveable when I am competent. If I am not competent, I don't deserve to even live. Competence is, therefore, essential for survival. I defend my competence at any turn. If I feel I appear incompetent, I will vigorously defend myself and then follow that up with a huge effort to ensure I am competent. Worse still, I will attempt to make others look incompetent, as it makes me look more competent. As you can imagine, I have inflicted significant pain on others, both family and colleagues, through this approach.

Each of us has our own version of belief patterns. Each of us looks at the world through our own 'window' of beliefs, and we all think that this represents reality, not realising that everyone else is looking through a different window and has their own reality—a recipe for misunderstanding and underperformance.

The fact that women undervalue themselves by 20 per cent is yet another example of looking through our own window of reality. There is significant research that shows low-power groups attribute greater virtues to high-power groups than they do to themselves. It is as if the uneven playing field has been replicated within the mindset causing a double whammy of an external <u>and</u> internal uneven playing field.

The good news is that we can reprogram our beliefs and replace them with beliefs that reduce depression, anxiety and limiting mindsets so we can improve our performance and increase our happiness and satisfaction. Think of our brain as being like a computer running software of beliefs and values—we can reprogram the application.

HISTORY

Our history, childhood and life experiences have a profound impact on our mindset and hence our long-term health, well-being and achievements in life.

PARENTING MATTERS

Our mindset is the product of what we've inherited: our genes, life experiences, and most importantly, childhood memories. Our childhood matters; it is a key determinant of our mindset today. It is suggested that from the ages 0–7, a child absorbs everything around them as a fact. If, in this period, a child is told that they are bad, they are likely to internalise that as a fact. Former editor and publisher of *Mothering* magazine,

Peggy O'Mara, says, 'Be careful how you speak to your children, one day it will become their inner voice.' During childhood, we pick up the majority of our values, traits and thinking patterns from our parents. We are sponges, programming our brains in line with those of our parents.

Many people in our community today suffer from some version of *I'm not good enough*. This *I'm not good enough* thinking pattern is debilitating and prevents us achieving our full potential. It sits as a constant critic inside our head, which not only limits our potential, but severely diminishes our enjoyment of life. How can you enjoy having a conversation with a handsome young man, who's obviously interested in you, if you believe that you're ugly, fat or not good enough? How can you put your best foot forward in a job interview, if you think you're not up to the role or promotion?

There is absolutely no doubt that the way we were raised has a significant impact on our mindset and life outcomes. The Adverse Childhood Experiences (ACE) study shows that the psychological impact of trauma in childhood can have a massive impact on the long-term mental and physical health of those children as they become adults. An 'ACE' is a specific example of a childhood trauma. Examples of an 'ACE' include physical, verbal or sexual abuse, and emotional neglect. Other examples of an ACE include having a parent who is an alcoholic or a victim of domestic violence. The study reported that 67 per cent of Americans experienced at least one ACE in their childhood. The study found that those with an ACE score of 4 were 12 times more likely to attempt suicide, and 7.5 times more likely to become alcoholic or to use illicit drugs (Centers for Disease Control and Prevention, 2016). The best predictor of long-term mental and physical health is childhood experiences.

For those of us who have experienced adverse childhood experiences, this study provides clear evidence that it does impact our future. For those of us who haven't experienced an ACE, it's not hard to imagine that many of those mini-traumas carried throughout childhood can still have an impact on our mindset. I don't declare that we should blame our childhoods for everything that's wrong today, but processing our history allows us to put the negative impact behind us so we can reach our full potential. Understanding of the importance of a childhood can also help parents raise children with stronger and more resilient mindsets.

Jenny Law

Jenny grew up in country Victoria. She went to Monash University and studied a combined degree in Japanese and Materials Engineering. She graduated in the middle of Australia's last recession, in the early 1990s, but managed to land a role with Industrial Noise Control, which manufactured soundproofing materials.

She then landed a great job at Nissan Casting Australia, which manufactures aluminum automotive engine parts. At the time, the demand for aluminum componentry was continuing to grow strongly as part of efforts to lighten the weight of cars. There was also significant government investment in R&D, where Jenny became Coordinator.

Jenny started her family in her late 20s and went on to have three boys. Nissan Casting were very accommodating and enabled Jenny to work part-time. In the meantime, she and her husband were establishing a business called Megasorber, that designed and manufactured noise control materials for a range of industries, including residential and commercial building applications, soundproofing around generators and engines.

Eventually Jenny resigned from Nissan Casting, and she now works full time at Megasorber, which, being her own company, enables her the flexibility she wants to enable her to spend time with her boys, work on her business, and significantly contribute to the community—which she does in multiple ways.

Jenny is unassuming, unpretentious, and highly capable. She's also extremely generous, including allowing me to use Megasorber's training rooms at no cost when I was first establishing my parenting business. She was so highly regarded at Nissan Casting that they still ask her to work on projects for them. It's a credit to Nissan Casting that they were able to support Jenny while she was establishing her family.

BEING RAISED AS A GIRL

There are a huge number of cultural influences on who we become, our beliefs, values and mindset. So it is no big surprise that there is a gender dimension to the mindset story. Tara Mohr, in her book

Playing Big. points out that women are particularly sensitive to criticism and are 'hooked' on praise. Tara argues that women's heightened sensitivity tends to lead women to 'play small' from fear of criticism.

Tara describes six possible causes of this sensitivity in women:

- higher rating of the importance of relationships.

- cultural focus on the appearance of women.

- history of survival through 'being liked'. Lack of own resources requiring dependency on others.

- heightened awareness of the reactions of others.

- fear of personal attacks that appear so frequently in the media, e.g. Hillary Clinton.

- 'good girl' conditioning.

Good girl conditioning is the cultural expectation of girls to be kind, quite, considerate, and likable. Don't be loud, aggressive or draw attention to yourself. Obviously, this is not the list of traits normally associated with leadership.

The conditioning of girls at school reinforces these mindsets. It is so much easier for girls to sit quietly and concentrate on their schoolwork compared to boys who have trouble concentrating and sitting still. Girls are rewarded for their 'good behaviour' by teachers who constantly praise them, leading to girls growing up 'hooked on praise'. Raising children using excessive praise causes a range of mindset and self-esteem problems. It encourages children to look externally for feelings of self-worth rather than relying on their own judgements of their performance. Praising children when the praise does not match their views of their self-worth will lead to lower self-esteem and confidence. Girls seem to be more at risk of the 'damage of praise' than boys are—they get more of it because they tend to behave in a more socially acceptable manner than boys.

Being good performers at school can lead to belief systems and life-long habits that work in the education system but don't necessarily work in life, especially if you aspire to leadership roles. Success at school is the result of working hard and keeping the teacher happy. You learn that if you work hard and get good grades you will do well. You assume that if you work hard and do well in your job that you will also do well. The rules at work are different.

The things you learned at school did not set you up well for leadership in the workplace. Leadership requires that you challenge and influence authority, not just defer to it. Working hard can lead to over-preparation to 'get it right', which can simply be impossible to achieve, lead to chronic overwork, and does not allow for the development of the skills of improvisation or 'thinking on your feet', critical for leadership. Working hard to 'please the teacher' does not give you the necessary skills to enable what you achieve at work to be visible and make you promotable.

GROWTH VS FIXED MINDSET

We develop either a fixed or a growth mindset depending on our childhood and parenting. A person with a fixed mindset believes they have a fixed ability that needs to be proven, where a person with a growth mindset believes ability can be developed through learning (Dweck, 2012).

A child with a fixed mindset believes their abilities are innate, and so won't work hard to make improvements. A child who is told they are clever believes this to be a desirable characteristic and they will be lovable when they are clever. If they are not clever, they are somehow less worthy or less lovable, and will do anything to prove the opposite. Forty per cent of students with a fixed mindset are capable of lying in order to 'prove' their capabilities (Dweck, 2012). Our mindset is likely determined by the way we are raised. Being continually told how cleaver we are as children is likely to develop a fixed mindset.

Adam Guettel, (grandson of Richard Rogers, who wrote the music for *Oklahoma*) was considered to be gifted. but failed to reach any potential because he was riddled with anxiety and fear of failure. 'In my family, to be good is to fail, to be very good is to fail. The only thing that is not failure is to be great.' Clearly, he felt he was unable to be great. It is possible James Hird has a fixed mindset and needed to prove he truly was the 'golden-haired boy', and be as successful as a coach as he was a player. In order to ensure his success as a coach he 'pushed the boundaries' of the drug code with disastrous results at the Essendon Football Club. Not just for himself, but for all of the players who experienced one-year bans, and for Jobe Watson who lost his Brownlow Medal.

Luckily, thanks to neuroplasticity, we can change our mindsets and develop a growth mindset. Here are my top five favourite tips for developing a growth mindset:

1. Remember that we are always in learning.

2. See your activities as an experiment. In an experiment, there is no failure, just data.

3. Use the word yet. *It's not that I can't do something, it's just that I can't do something, yet.*

4. Put in the effort. Remember that effort counts more than talent.

5. Reward yourself for your inputs. You do not have full control over the outcomes, but you do have full control over the input and the effort that you put into achieving that outcome, so reward them rather than rewarding the outcome.

HEALING AND HIGH PERFORMANCE

Everyone has 'trauma' to heal whether they be minor upsets or major challenges of neglect and abuse from childhood. Healing is essential so our mindsets can be further enhanced for high performance. Here is a summary of options:

EYE MOVEMENT DESENSITISATION AND REPROCESSING (EMDR)

EMDR is a process that has been rigorously studied by the US Army and is used extensively to help treat post-traumatic stress syndrome. EMDR is also used to treat victims of childhood abuse and trauma to great effect.

Bessel van der Kolk (2014) has documented this methodology in his book *The Body Keeps the Score: Mind, Brain, and Body in the Healing of Trauma*. Van der Kolk describes how traditional talk therapies, such as counselling, is quite ineffective and can be traumatising for those people who have experienced severe abuse. The EMDR method works on the principle that our memories are stored in our body, and although we can't change what happened to us, we can change the intensity of our memories and how we interpret them. It's a bit like taking a photograph of a childhood memory, photo-shopping it, pixelating it, turning it black and white, and making it blurry until it fades into the distance. EMDR practitioners exist. They are properly certified, safe, and reliable, and have a sound theoretical basis.

THE HOFFMAN PROCESS

The Hoffman Quadrinity Process is an intense, ten-day process where you review, reframe, and understand your childhood; this leads to greater integration of all four elements of ourselves: our body, mind, emotions, and spirit. I participated in this process fifteen years ago. I had a perfectly normal childhood with no ACEs. I liken this process to a second opportunity to grow into a more integrated and mature human being. After completing this process, my capabilities dramatically improved and I went from being close to failing in my general management role to excelling in it, primarily because I removed many unproductive self-beliefs and behaviours that existed as defence mechanisms, to enable me to feel okay about myself.

TIME-LINE

Time-Line is a remarkably simple visualisation process, which again, takes a memory and reprocesses it to remove intensity. I have used this process with at least two-thirds of my leadership coaching clients. I am constantly amazed at how high functioning executives still struggle with emotional reactions to situations that have their roots in childhood. I had one client who was having a severe emotional response to a perceived emotion inside his organisation. He was responding badly, behaving badly, and at risk of throwing away a sound career. He was reliving a situation experienced over twenty years ago, and his emotional response was connected to feeling stupid and incapable at school. A simple visualisation process can take the intensity out of such experiences and reduce the negative responses that happen in our current lives. This process works along the same lines as the EMDR process, where the goal is to change the intensity of the memory so it has less impact on us.

LANDMARK EDUCATION

The Landmark Forum is a 3-day intensive program that provides people with an understanding of the basic structures of how they think and behave. Landmark philosophy predicates that we have a 'view of life', which creates our own reality—there is no truth. This view of life influences how we live. How our life pans out is fundamentally a result of our view of life. Landmark is based on transformative or experimental learning and is a different educational experience than learning knowledge in traditional education. Landmark is a program for those who want to be more effective in their lives and less limited by their beliefs. It is also very helpful for those who are experiencing anxiety or depression.

MINDSET HYGIENE

Mindset hygiene is about managing your thoughts. Thoughts are actually real. For centuries, Yogis have talked about the importance of thoughts, and now science is catching up. Psychiatrist and author Daniel G. Amen, says, 'Did you know that every thought you have sends electrical signals throughout your brain? Thoughts have actual physical properties. They are real. They have significant influence on every cell of your body.' (Amen D. D., 1999). Not only are thoughts real—thoughts matter. Our thoughts are the blueprints for our behaviour. Everything we do, we do twice; first, in our head as a thought and then as a behaviour or an action.

Mastery of thoughts can make the world of difference in your ability to survive the rough-and-tumble of working in a male-dominated environment. In this section, we're going to discuss various ways we can manage the hygiene of our thoughts and thinking patterns for greater effectiveness.

PARADIGMS

It's useful to understand the mental paradigms, or world views within which we operate. They provide frameworks for our beliefs and our thoughts to sit within. I imagine a paradigm as a pair of glasses with a particular coloured lens, through which I view the world. When I change the colour of the lens, the world looks different. Paradigm means a pattern, model or a generally-accepted perspective. I have always operated within a paradigm that I should focus on my career, save up enough money to retire comfortably and then enjoy the world. Then, in the middle of the global financial crisis, everything that could go wrong, did go wrong and my career imploded. I was out of work with a 4-year-old at home. When he started school, I started job hunting, looking for similar general manager roles I'd held previously. I couldn't land the right role. I thought hard about taking junior roles but was unconvinced that would work. Emotionally, I was hurting. I was humiliated. I felt hopeless. I was worried about my future. Every month that I wasn't earning, I felt my future was fading away. Through much soul searching, I decided to 'try on' a different paradigm. My new paradigm was that I existed to learn to be the best person I could, and to serve others. I adopted the belief that whatever happened was an opportunity to learn; hence it didn't matter if something bad happened because it was all part of that learning opportunity.

When I viewed the world through paradigm A, I became anxious and worried about the future; but looking via paradigm B, I relaxed and accepted whatever was happening to me as being okay, and something I could manage.

Useful paradigms would be *life is a journey*; it's about what we do on the journey rather than the destination. It is what we learn, not what we earn that matters—a life lived through service to others and gratitude for what we have. Unhelpful paradigms are thinking that the more material possessions we have the happier we will be; that what others think is important; that to be okay, we have to be perfect.

I invite you to explore and understand what your paradigms are. Which ones are unique to you? Which ones did you learn from your parents? Which ones are society-wide paradigms? What paradigms do you hold that serve you, and what ones do you hold that don't serve you? Which ones make you happy and which ones improve service to others?

REALITY IS NOT REAL

We all see 'reality'. Unfortunately, what we think is reality is not actually real. Let me explain. I grew up in Melbourne but found myself living in Perth for a few years; my younger sister was also living there at the time. We would catch up for lunch and sometimes talk about our childhood. At the time I was suffering depression and was undergoing counselling. While I listened to my sister talk about her childhood I became more and more intrigued. She had a different perception of shared events (with the same parents). She was the youngest and I was the eldest, which did mean that things would have been a bit different. But I began to wonder if we had actually grown up in the same house and had the same parents!

Remember the multi-coloured glasses I mentioned earlier? Well imagine that everyone is wearing their own coloured glasses. When we look at what happened in any given event we actually record reality differently. There are as many different records of reality as there are observers to an event.

So where does our reality come from? It comes from the stories that we make up about life, how it is or should be. Let me give you an example. When I was a child I used to help mum clean up after camping while my sisters were doing other things. My mum gave me a wonderful compliment about how competent and capable I was (the actual words I cannot remember). At that moment, I made a decision, which changed my life and the tint on my glasses. I decided that if I were competent I was lovable. From this came many other 'logical' deductions. If I were lovable then I was competent and, clearly, if I were incompetent, I was not lovable! I also had it in my head that if I were not lovable then I did not deserve to live. Hence, my value on the planet was linked to my feelings of competency. I was invested in 'being competent' – my very survival. I became obsessed with being competent. How about three university degrees! I made huge efforts at work to 'look good'. I was extremely sensitive to criticism – after all, if I was seen to be incompetent then I didn't deserve to live. The ugliest manifestation of this 'story that I made up in my head' was that I looked competent when others looked incompetent. So I took opportunities to make others look incompetent. Ouch!

One of the distinctions in LandMark Education is that of 'running a racket'. A racket is a story we have made up that has some sort of 'payoff'. For example, if I hold the view that my mother-in-law is a bitch (just for the record, in case my mother-in-law is reading this, I don't hold that view!) then I would be constantly looking for evidence to support my view; after all, we all want to be 'right'. So I would be looking at my mother-in-law through my 'mother-in-law is a bitch' set of glasses. It would not matter what she did, I would be able to use her behaviour to prove that she was a bitch. So what is the payoff? The payoff is that I can complain to my friends and they would give me sympathy. I could complain to my husband and feel self-righteous. I could avoid my duty to treat her with respect. After all, why would I respect someone who did not deserve it!

Uncovering and giving up your rackets is very powerful.

I was extremely fortunate to have worked at Yarra Valley Water when Landmark was introduced to the whole organisation. There was an individual in the organisation called David, whom I held in low regard. He thought I was an unpleasant human being who had been 'over-promoted'. I took every opportunity to demean him to others, which damaged him and me. I had to put much effort into avoiding him and avoiding working with him. Clearly getting anything productive done together was out of the question. No doubt he exhibited similar damaging and dysfunctional behaviours towards me. When we both learned about the concept of a 'racket', in the same training program, we were able to sit down together and declare, 'I'm running a racket about you'. Open and honest conversation enabled the racket to be dissolved and be replaced by a quality relationship, enhancing us both and dramatically improving our productivity in relation to each other. You can image the power of building such quality relationships across the organisation for dramatic improvements in productivity and individual health and well-being. As a result, Yarra Valley Water has one of the most constructive cultures globally as measured by *Human Synergistics* with their well-known Organisation Culture Inventory (OCI) tool.

So where you have an upset or complaint look for your own stories and rackets and remember that 'reality is not real'.

INNER VOICE – INNER CRITIC

All of us have an internal commentator commenting on everything that is going on in our lives, second-by-second, minute-by-minute and hour-by-hour. This commentator is not you, even though you think it is.

Perhaps having an internal commentator would be fine if they were your cheerleader *'hey well done for getting out of bed early, it's going to be a great day, what a yummy breakfast this is and look at what healthy food choices you have made. Going to the gym is easy and you look awesome in your old gym gear. You are so strong too! Wow look at what heavy weights you are lifting and look at how many calories you just burnt on the spin bike. There is hardly any traffic on the road on the way home and you only had to stop for six red lights over the 3km drive home. When you get home you husband is going to remind you of how much he loves you and you know he adores every fibre of your body.'*

Not sure about you, but my inner voice doesn't provide this type of commentary. It is more like, *'get out of bed. You should have got up earlier. Stop being lazy and get to the gym; it's no wonder you are overweight. OMG look at the bags under your eyes and your skin is looking blotchy again and your hair is still dry even after spending a ridiculous amount of money on that hair conditioner. You really should comb your hair before going to the gym; it's a mess. You have served up too much breakfast and over-eaten again. Now you have to make three meals at once, breakfast for you, breakfast for Rhys and then Rhys' school lunch – so not fair. Why doesn't your husband make a bigger effort? Just more proof that he does not love you and, therefore, you are not all that lovable. Something is wrong with you, and you don't even know what it is.'*

Welcome to your inner critic. Your inner critic is the endless voice inside you that provides ongoing critical commentary. Your inner critic can be harsh and unreasonable. Your inner critic speaks to you in ways that you would never speak to another person. Your inner critic is constantly comparing you to the 'perfect person' who clearly does not exist—even on the front of magazines.

So what is your inner critic trying to do? Sabotage your life? Actually, your inner critic exists to keep you safe. It evolved to stop you from getting killed. It evolved to say, *'don't walk over there: what if there is a snake in the grass. Don't speak to that stranger, they might kill you. Watch out for lions'*. Walking down the street in our modern life does not get us killed. But the inner critic interprets unhappy-looking people, and things you have not done before, as existential risks and it warns you of the dangers. Your inner critic is trying to keep you safe. Instead, it is causing you anxiety and preventing you from living a full life— from doing things in life that involve taking risks.

So what can you do about it? First, you cannot turn off your inner critic. Abusing and ignoring your inner critic will not help. But you can make friends with it. When you are about to do something new and a bit scary, listen to it, thank it for its advice and then make your own decisions on how to proceed.

FEAR

Fear is debilitating and without doubt it prevents us from achieving to our full potential. It also dramatically reduces our well-being and enjoyment of life. Anxiety, which is an extended stress response that remains after the initial trigger is over, is estimated to affect one in four Australians at some time in their life with a gender bias of one-in-three women and one-in-five men.

So what is fear, and why does it exist? Our ability to feel fear keeps us safe. Fear prevents us from doing dangerous things and avoiding dangerous circumstances. When we feel fear, the brain responds in two ways. A message is sent to the reptilian part of our brain that controls our fight or flight response – the amygdala. This releases the stress hormone cortisol and quickly mobilises the body to run or fight. Our heart-rate increases and we will react according to our basic instincts, which is to 'flight or fight'. This message route is sometimes called the 'low road'. At the same time, a message is sent via the 'high road', to the neocortex, the rational part of the brain. The neocortex looks for a rational response to the threat and makes a rational decision. Many times the neocortex is able to assess the threat, discover it is non-threatening and send a message to the amygdala to 'stand down'.

We are all born with two fears: a fear of falling and a fear of loud noises. The rest of our fears are learned, from our parents or life experiences. Natural fears, like fears of spiders and snakes, are learned from parents and passed down through the generations – after all, many snakes and spiders are poisonous. However, many learned fears are not rational but are still passed on.

Although fear helped keep us safe in prehistoric times, sabre-toothed tigers are not strolling through our cities today. In fact, we have wiped out most animals with the capacity to eat us. Our fear mechanisms, that once kept us safe, are mal-adapted for our modern society and are over-reactive. There is no existential threat from standing up in front of a group of people to speak, or from sitting an exam. Yet our fear responses are triggered. There can be significant benefit to us from learning methods to 'turn down the fear'.

We can learn many ways to manage fear responses. One of the most important is to expose ourselves to the fear. The more we experience the fearful situation, the more practice the brain has at responding with the 'high road' rather than the 'low road'. This also gives the neocortex practice at calming ourselves down.

I fly a paraglider. I learned to fly about 12 years ago, and it still scares me. I used to get scared because of the height, but now when I take off I just get an adrenalin rush. I know that I can launch and land my glider safely, but I developed a fear of thermic (rough) air (when warm air moving upwards and cool airs moving downwards). The more time I spend in rough air, the less fearful I become and the more I enjoy my flying.

Jia Jiang has a great TED talk called *What I learned from 100 days of rejection*. Fear of rejection originated from an unpleasant childhood experience and had become a major 'hand-brake' on achieving his life goals. He undertook a regime of exposure therapy, which involved deliberately exposing himself to rejection for 100 days in a row to discover that his fear could be conquered.

Rationalising with ourselves is also helpful. Asking 'what is the worst thing that can happen if this goes wrong' can be very useful. For example, what is the worst thing that could happen if you put yourself forward for a job? You won't get it. Any distressing emotions that arise can be dealt with.

Anxiety or worry is a form of 'imagined fear' that is unique to humans. Our wonderful neocortex enables us to rationalise, but it also enables us to plan the future. We use this to think about all the things that could go wrong which triggers a fear response. Our brain can self-generate fears without them actually occurring in the outside world. No doubt this is the basis of constant worry and anxiety.

Being 'in the moment' is a strong antidote for anxiety because when we are 'in the moment' we are not imagining what could go wrong. Thinking about the past involves guilt, and thinking about the future evokes fear. The only place of peace is by being 'in the moment'. It is for this reason that meditation and mindfulness are such great tools for managing anxiety. We discuss this more in the next section: Mindset Habits. Other techniques for 'being in the moment' include tapping into our bodies through breathing or exercise. When I am practising karate, I am always in the moment—my brain is being totally engaged executing karate.

Tara Mohr calls these types of fear 'Pachad'. But she also describes another type of fear: 'Yirah'. According to Tara, Yirah has three different meanings. It is:

- the feeling that overcomes us when we inhabit a larger space than we are used to.

- the feeling we experience when we suddenly come into possession of considerably more energy than we had before.

- what we feel in the presence of the divine.

I think that Yirah is what I experience when I launch my paraglider. Feelings of excitement and exhilaration mixed with fear, and the thrill mixed with fear when I stand in front of an audience.

When you learn to determine whether you are feeling Pachad or Yirah, you can calm yourself. If it is Yirah then you know that you are heading in the right direction—keep pursuing your goals.

REFRAMING

Sometimes, bad things happen, and our memories of those experiences impact our decisions. When my son was two, a little white scotty dog jumped on him; its nose was in his face. My son is older now and he loves dogs, except little white scotty dogs. His experience with this type of dog influenced him and his memory. It's not the event that matters; it's how we remember it. There are simple techniques for reframing events and changing our memories of them.

When I was 14, I thought I had a big bum, and I was mortified when one of my school friends told me so. I covered up with baggy t-shirts, which made me look big overall; they turned me into a beach ball. I have learned now, at the age of 52, to tuck in my shirts and celebrate my curves, rather than worrying about my big bum.

How can we deal with, or reframe, memories that impact our lives, many of which we're not even conscious of? The answer is remarkably simple: take that image, and change the way it looks. Pixelate it, turn it black and white, make it blurry. If it's a sound, make it resemble Donald Duck. I was once involved in a misunderstanding with a client, which caused her to be angry at me. I was upset because I had tried so hard to look after her; I apologised to her, but she refused to accept my apology. I walked out of our meeting, quite upset, and could easily have let the encounter wreck my whole day. I thought to myself, *There is no way I'm going to let this wreck my whole day*. I replayed the scene in my head. This time, I made her voice sound silly—like Donald Duck. This took out the emotional sting of the event and I got on with my day.

OPPOSING NEGATIVE THINKING

As we discussed earlier, our thoughts really do matter; they are real and they cause physiological responses. Many of us suffer from automatic negative thinking (ANT). Having one or two ANTs at your picnic is not too much of a problem, but when you're living in the metaphoric ANT nest—life is pretty unpleasant. Negative thoughts create negative behaviours and dramatically undermine their productivity. As a female, doing it tough in the engineering sector, we require resilience against an ANT invasion.

Daniel Amen suggests we develop ANTeaters to deal with ANTS; whenever you notice an ANT entering your mind, you train yourself to recognise it and run it down. Then, talk back to them. As you talk back to your thoughts, you take away some of the negative power and gain control over your mood. People suffering from the *I'm not good enough* belief pattern could replace that thought with *I'm doing the best I can with what I've got and I'm going to give life a real hard go*.

EXPECTATIONS AND COMPARISONS

No discussion on the hygiene of our thoughts would be complete without talking about expectations and comparisons. Holding expectations and making constant comparisons with other people are a short cut to misery and disappointment. Our inner critic is constantly comparing us to the 'perfect person' who does not exist in reality. The perfect person is a concoction of all of the attributes we admire in others. Attributes that have been distorted through Facebook and airbrushed by fashion editors. When our feelings of self-worth are dependent on how we measure up to some other person or to the 'perfect' person, we will always be disappointed. We are guaranteed to fail. When we compare how things turned out with how we expected them to turn out, we will also be disappointed.

MENTAL HEALTH HABITS

We need habits for a healthy mind, just as we do for a healthy body. Such habits can help relieve anxiety and depression, and are essential for high performance.

AUTHENTICITY

Truly understanding and expressing who you are is one of the most productive and satisfying lifelong habits you can develop for a healthy and productive mindset.

'Everything will line up perfectly when knowing and living the truth becomes more important than looking good.'—Alan Cohen, author of 24 books including *The Dragon Doesn't Live Here Anymore.*

Authenticity is particularly challenging in today's society when we spend so much of our time trying to 'look good'. This obsession with 'looking good' drives us to pretend that things are different from what they really are. And this slippery slope leads us to be more dishonest. It is not hard to fall into the trap of lying—just to look good. Every time we lie or lack authenticity, we diminish ourselves. French philosopher, Michel de Montaigne says, 'I do myself a greater injury in lying than I do him of whom I tell a lie.'

A lack of authenticity also dramatically reduces the influence and effectiveness of our communications. People have great 'bullshit detectors'. Your lack of authenticity will push them away from you. They won't trust you. If you are in sales they certainty won't buy from you. People are drawn to those people who authentically express who they are.

Being authentic sounds easy and obvious. Children are completely authentic. What you see is what you get. So why do we have this crisis of authenticity? We live in a world of advertising and media that is constantly sending us messages as to what 'perfect' looks like, and what we should look like to be acceptable. It took me years to realise that if I was rejected in a job application process, it was not because 'there was something wrong with me', it was because a job application process was about matching the right person for the right role. Instead, I asked 'how do I change myself?' in order for me to fit in to what people want. Every time I did this I became less authentic, I lost a part of my true self, and I became less influential.

'Be yourself – everyone else is already taken.'—Oscar Wilde

INNER MENTOR

In the chapter on hygiene we talked about the inner critic. In fact, we also have an inner mentor – it is just that she is not nearly as vocal as the inner critic. We are constantly being encouraged to seek mentors. However, the experience of women getting good mentors is poor. Women describe being unable to find good mentors, not getting good advice from mentors or being cut down or diminished by someone you considered as a mentor. Our best mentor, the one that truly knows what we need and want is our inner mentor. Tara Mohr says, 'The inner mentor is an imagined version of an older, wiser you—you twenty years out into the future. Once you have a vivid sense of this older, wiser, more authentic version of yourself, you'll find that she exists as a voice within you right now.' Tara provides a great meditation that enables us to connect with our inner mentor and can be found in her book, *Playing Big*.

Once we connect with our inner mentor, we can consult with her at any time we please by 'tuning in' and asking her what she would do in the current circumstances. As we age and mature, and listen to our inner mentor, we 'grow into her'.

So if you have a good mentor or if you find one, then use them. We learn from others. But take their advice as 'pieces of data' to inform your decisions, not as advice that should be followed. There is only one person who truly knows who you are, what you need and what you value – and that person is you.

DEALING WITH FEEDBACK

One of the most useful habits you can learn is to 'filter feedback'. As part of our external perspective and desires to fit in and look good, we are constantly seeking feedback on ourselves. We are constantly being urged to seek and act on feedback. Don't get me wrong, feedback can be useful and essential if we want to be effective in the world. But it is just data, not a reflection of your personal value. Feedback says more about the other person than it says about you. Be selective from whom and where you seek feedback. Ask yourself 'do I need to take on this feedback? Will taking on this feedback really make my work significantly better? Does this feedback say more about them than me?'

Dealing with negative feedback can be quite damaging. I will never forget the first time I got a 360-degree feedback on my leadership performance. I was devastated. It took me six months to recover from my feelings of hurt and rejection. Yes, I got some useful data but at a high price, in that my confidence and feelings of self-worth were damaged. When I shared the idea of filtering feedback with one of my clients, she realised that the feedback she had been given about her appearance and recommendations that she 'use some lipstick' said more about the other person than it did about her. This enabled her to be free to make her own decisions.

Think about your target market. Whether it be your boss or potential clients, your work must resonate with them, not with anyone else. If you try to please everyone you will end up pleasing no one. Your family's view of your work may be completely irrelevant (if they are not your target market).

DEALING WITH DARK TIMES

We all go through dark times—when things don't quite work out how we want them to. How do we maintain our enthusiasm and regain our mojo?

There is a saying, 'God only shows you the next step'. You are on a journey of life and learning; however, you cannot see the full journey, only the next step. You have to take that step otherwise you will stay stuck. In summary, just do something that speaks to you and has you learning. You never know where it will take you.

MINDFULLNESS AND MEDITATION

We can incorporate many helpful habits into our lives to improve our mental well-being. By far, the most popular and effective are mindfulness and meditation.

Meditation is a formal process of sitting and focusing on just one thing, for example, the breath or a mantra. Mindfulness is the process of bringing one's attention fully to whatever one is doing in the moment. For example, we can wash the dishes mindfully, by noticing how the light reflects off the plates or by observing how the foam moves in the sink. There is no end to the list of benefits one can get from mindfulness and meditation. Scientific and medical research continues to show huge benefits in many areas of our lives, especially when it comes to our mental health. Yoga is another daily habit used by millions of people to help manage their mindset. Yoga is a version of mindfulness and meditation, where we focus on the movement of our body. I have taken up Karate and love it. I realised that Karate is a mindfulness exercise. When I am practising or learning a new block, punch or kick, I am totally focused on my body and have to be 'in the moment'. It is impossible for me to think about what to cook for dinner or worry about the meeting I had that day, when I am so focused.

HEART-BREATHING

I incorporate heart breathing into my daily routine. This process is based on the work of the HeartMath Institute. The HeartMath Institute studies the connection between the brain and the heart. It has identified neurological material in both organs implying that the heart is a mini brain. The HeartMath Institute provides tools and techniques to enable the heart and brain to work in synch to reduce stress levels. A simple technique from the institute is to shut your eyes and imagine you are breathing in and out through your heart. I teach this practice to coaching clients. In less than a minute, you can actually feel the relaxation throughout the room.

EXERCISE

Physical exercise releases endorphins for a healthy mind, and strengthens the body for maximum performance. There are many possible exercise habits, chose one that works for you, and incorporate it into your daily routine. Exercise is non-negotiable. Even walking helps. Just move your body.

Chapter 6

SERVICE TO OTHER WOMEN

MEAN WOMEN

While writing this book, I have reflected much on my own career experiences. I discovered that my career has been filled with meeting wonderful women and has been impacted by interactions with thoroughly unpleasant women. I reflected heavily on what my role in eliciting negative reactions from some other women might have been, and concluded that although I can be grumpy and lack diplomacy there was something else going on. As research for this book, I decided to investigate this phenomenon and discover why mean women exist in the engineering sector. I came across the term *relationship abuse*, which is what women do to other women. It's the official term for 'bitchiness' or 'cattiness'. It seems that relationship abuse is not exclusive to women, but far more common.

There is a range of theories as to why women participate in this type of behaviour. The one that stands out most, for the purpose of this book, is that women are far more *relationship orientated* than men. Women, act out their aggression emotionally rather than physically—they act it out through their relationships. Relationship abuse is aggression perpetrated through the relationship. It is far more common in adolescents than older women. But some mean girls in the schoolyard grow up and exhibit the same behaviour in the corporate world or in social circles. Additionally, when you've been the only woman in your sector for a long time, and you have felt special because of this, it wouldn't feel so glorious when more women join you, particularly if you never had support during your career.

COPING WITH MEAN WOMEN

What do we do about relationship abuse? First, you need to recognise that it happens, then you can depersonalise it. The women who perpetrate relationship abuse clearly have problems of their own, and when they perpetrate relationship abuse, it's more about them then it is about you. Don't take it personally. However, psychological wounds, which can be experienced at any stage of our lives, require healing.

I was shocked, recently, when an HR director, whom I'd just met, berated and humiliated me in front one of her colleagues and a connection of mine. I was deeply shocked and hurt, and I had to process it in my mind. I recognised that it was all about her and not about me; this helped me depersonalise it and take away some of the sting.

The corporate world, with its layers and power structures, can be fertile ground for women who want to perpetuate relationship abuse.

'There's a special place in hell for women who don't help other women.'—Madeleine Albright

My credo for supporting other women is:

1. We're on this planet to make a difference and to serve others.

2. Treat other people as if they were your boss.

3. Go out of your way to support other women in the engineering sector.

Supporting other women in male-dominated workplaces is critical. Unfortunately, for some reason that I cannot explain, women who have 'made it' in male-dominated environments are not necessarily supportive or helpful to other women in that same environment.

During my early years as a graduate, I rarely met a senior woman. And the first three senior women I did meet were unpleasant and failed to provide any advice or support. It was extraordinarily disappointing; I took it personally, as I didn't yet have the maturity to realise that it wasn't about me, it was about them. Although my time with these women was more than 25 years ago, I'll never forget the debilitating effect of their actions. As a junior female engineer, it would have made the world of difference to have received some guidance, support, mentoring and just plain friendliness. I like to think that I haven't repeated their mistakes, but it's quite possible that I haven't done enough to reach out to younger women as I've progressed through my career.

CONCLUSION

Female engineers are gold. Never forget that. You have a powerful combination of analytical capability with the natural propensity to relationship capabilities. You've already invested in an engineering degree and established yourself in a career, then you may as well be the absolute best you can be and make the best contribution you possibly can. To do this, stay employed. If you don't choose to have a family or are unable to have a family, staying employed should be relatively easy. Even bouts of unemployment can be leveraged to build skills and identify other opportunities.

If you choose to have a family, again, stay employed. Utilise your maternity leave. Come back to work and get help. Ask for support to help you be a great parent; remember, it takes a village to raise a child—you don't have to do it on your own.

Remember the four key elements to curating confidence, and a great career and life:

1. Be clear on your *mission*. Understand what you want to do, why, and how you can make the greatest contribution.

2. Build your social *mastery*. You have all the technical skills you need and can easily obtain the ones you don't. Your ability to contribute and succeed will

depend on your relationship mastery and ability to lead teams.

3. Manage your *mindset*. Success in life has very little to do with IQ and everything to do with mindset and determination. If you're in any doubt about that, watch *Eddie the Eagle*—show it to your kids as well.

4. Finally, give it a go. Many women lack the confidence to really step up to be their best. The skills we've talked about in this book are all about building your confidence so you can step up, lean in and be the best you can be.

SURVEY DATA ANALYSIS

The survey was delivered to my database in June 2016 via LinkedIn. I received 127 responses. Overleaf are the results of the data analysis

HAVE YOU BEEN DISCRIMINATED AGAINST ON THE BASIS OF YOUR GENDER?

Rating	Response count (ALL)	Distribution	Response count (WITHOUT children)	Distribution	Response count (WITH children)	Distribution
Major (unwanted sexual advances)	7	5.69%	5	8.47%	2	3.13%
Major (you considered yourself bullied)	8	6.50%	3	5.08%	5	7.81%
Significant (you felt unwelcome in your workplace)	15	12.20%	6	10.17%	9	14.06%
Minor (the odd joke and sexist remark)	63	51.22%	33	55.93%	30	47.62%
No	16	13.01%	7	11.86%	9	14.06%
Others	14	11.38%	5	8.47%	9	14.06%
TOTAL	123		59		64	

HAVE YOUR CAREER OPPORTUNITIES BEEN LIMITED BASED ON GENDER?

Rating	Response count (ALL)	Distribution of Responders	Response count (WITHOUT children)	Distribution of Responders	Response count (WITH children)	Distribution of Responders
No	**34**	27.64%	23	39.98%	11	17.19%
Possibly	**46**	37.40%	20	33.90%	26	40.63%
Probably	**24**	19.51%	11	18.64%	13	20.31%
Yes	**16**	13.01%	3	5.08%	13	20.31%
Comment	**3**	2.44%	2	3.39%	1	1.64%
TOTAL	**123**		**59**		**64**	

AVERAGES FOR ALL RATINGS (WITH OR WITHOUT CHILDREN)

| | Count | PAST EMPLOYMENT | | CURRENT EMPLOYMENT | | | | | | FUTURE EMPLOYMENT | |
		Satisfaction	Development Opportunities	Satisfaction	Development Opportunities	Training	Culture	Flexibility		Existing Firm	Other Firm
All	**123**	**3.740**	**3.382**	**3.800**	**3.553**	**3.326**	**3.837**	**3.910**		**3.480**	**3.420**
Women WITHOUT children	59	3.814	3.441	3.780	3.593	3.288	3.814	3.847		3.559	3.729
Women WITH children	64	3.672	3.328	3.828	3.516	3.188	3.859	3.969		3.406	3.141

AVERAGES

AVERAGES FOR ALL RATINGS (BASED ON AGE GROUP)

	Count	Distribution	PAST EMPLOYMENT		CURRENT EMPLOYMENT					FUTURE EMPLOYMENT	
			Satisfaction	Development Opportunities	Satisfaction	Development Opportunities	Training	Culture	Flexibility	Existing Firm	Other Firm
All	123		3.740	3.382	3.800	3.553	3.326	3.837	3.910	3.480	3.420
20-30 yo	39	31.71%	3.641	3.385	3.821	3.795	3.538	4.051	3.821	3.769	3.692
31-40 yo	46	37.40%	3.761	3.283	3.739	3.348	2.848	3.674	3.848	3.261	3.457
41-50 yo	33	26.83%	3.788	3.485	3.848	3.545	3.515	3.848	4.061	3.424	3.182
51 yo up	5	4.07%	4.000	3.600	4.000	3.600	2.600	3.600	4.200	3.600	2.600

THUMBNAILS FOR TEAM ALIGNMENT

	Technical	People	Scheduling
CEO	• Develop and recommend strategy to the Board • Monitor strategy implementation • Ensure financial viability and does not run out of money • Ensure risk is understood and managed • Fundraise • Be spokesperson for the company • Manage key stakeholder and client relations • Ensure legal compliance • Lead the development and implementation of policies and systems	• Build, lead and integrate a team of direct reports capable of the work • Manage staff performance by setting clear accountabilities and authorities, goals, tasks, coaching, feedback • Undertake manager-once-removed accountabilities for talent management, career planning, succession planning, fair treatment and ensure competent and consistent leadership at all levels • Decide on removal of any company employees	• Schedule resources and assign tasks to ensure continuous workflow and fully loaded roles • Monitor and report on group business plans, financial, operational and improvement performance, including service level agreements

	Technical	People	Scheduling
CTO	• Identify technical solutions to market needs • Maintain relationships with key institutions • Technical spokesperson • Invent relevant technology • Advise CEO on recommended technology investments • Undertake relevant research to support production and future developments • Advise and support Engineering Group with technology • Develop, implement, manage and protect IP • Contribute to the development and management of risk	• Contribute to Executive teamwork on strategy, structure, systems and governance • Lead the implementation of policies and systems in own group • Build and lead a team of direct reports capable of the work • Manage staff performance by setting clear accountabilities and authorities, goals, tasks, coaching, feedback • Undertake manager-once-removed accountabilities for talent management, career planning, succession planning, fair treatment and ensuring competent and consistent leadership at all levels • Work collaboratively across the organisation	• Schedule resources and assign tasks to ensure continuous workflow and fully loaded roles • Monitor and report on group business plans, financial, operational and improvement performance, including service level agreements

	Technical	People	Scheduling
GM Product Development & Operations	• Develop a cost-effective and reliable product • Build production capacity • Execute and support new projects • Operations and maintenance • Licensee support (PD and Ops) • Customer support (PD and Ops) • Produce product • Develop and implement the quality management system • Manage the product development plans and processes • Develop and manage supply chain • Obtain and manage bankable data	• Contribute to Executive teamwork on strategy, structure, systems and governance • Lead the implementation of policies and systems in own group • Build and lead a team of direct reports capable of the work • Manage staff performance by setting clear accountabilities and authorities, goals, tasks, coaching, feedback • Undertake manager-once-removed accountabilities for talent management, career planning, succession planning, fair treatment and ensuring competent and consistent leadership at all levels • Work collaboratively across the organisation	• Schedule resources and assign tasks to ensure continuous workflow and fully loaded roles • Monitor and report on group business plans, financial, operational and improvement performance, including service level agreements

	Technical	People	Scheduling
CFO	• Developing corporate governance structures, delegated financial authority matrix • Recommend financial strategies to CEO • Advise CEO on financial matters • Assist CEO in capital raisings • Monitor financial indicators • Provide financial information to CEO • Meet company financial regulations • Provide data to peers to assist them in doing their jobs • Maintain integrity of accounting system • Treasury/cash management • Financial planning and budgeting and modelling • Develop a risk and insurance strategy • Company secretary • Company performance indicatory framework	• Contribute to Executive teamwork on strategy, structure, systems and governance • Lead the implementation of policies and systems in own group • Build and lead a team of direct reports capable of the work • Manage staff performance by setting clear accountabilities and authorities, goals, tasks, coaching, feedback • Undertake manager-once-removed accountabilities for talent management, career planning, succession planning, fair treatment and ensuring competent and consistent leadership at all levels • Work collaboratively across the organisation	• Schedule resources and assign tasks to ensure continuous workflow and fully loaded roles • Monitor and report on group business plans, financial, operational and improvement performance, including service level agreements

	Technical	People	Scheduling
CIO	• Recommend ICT strategy to CEO • Implement ICT strategy • Ensure suitable business systems • Monitor and maintain ICT systems • Ensure IP, network and data security • Provide ICT desktop support • Design, monitor and maintain suitable SCADA systems for plant • Ensure enterprise and product data availability and quality • Develop appropriate software for competitive advantage and to meet organisation's specific needs • Disaster recovery system • Operate Pilot Plant	• Contribute to Executive teamwork on strategy, structure, systems and governance • Lead the implementation of policies and systems in own group • Build and lead a team of direct reports capable of the work • Manage staff performance by setting clear accountabilities and authorities, goals, tasks, coaching, feedback • Undertake manager-once-removed accountabilities for talent management, career planning, succession planning, fair treatment and ensuring competent and consistent leadership at all levels • Work collaboratively across the organisation	• Schedule resources and assign tasks to ensure continuous workflow and fully loaded roles • Monitor and report on group business plans, financial, operational and improvement performance, including service level agreements

	Technical	People	Scheduling
GM Corporate Services	• Advise CEO on Human Resources matters • Support CEO to develop vibrant and productive organisational culture • Provide HR support to all staff and employees • Ensure appropriate HR framework, systems and processes are in place • Assist managers with induction and training of staff • Coordinating and providing employee training • Ensure compliance with IR law • Ensure suitable facilities are available to house staff and activities. • Provide general support to staff including cleaning, office supplies • Contract management • Development of an WH&S framework	• Contribute to Executive teamwork on strategy, structure, systems and governance • Lead the implementation of policies and systems in own group • Build and lead a team of direct reports capable of the work • Manage staff performance by setting clear accountabilities and authorities, goals, tasks, coaching, feedback • Undertake manager-once-removed accountabilities for talent management, career planning, succession planning, fair treatment and ensuring competent and consistent leadership at all levels • Work collaboratively across the organisation	• Schedule resources and assign tasks to ensure continuous workflow and fully loaded roles • Monitor and report on group business plans, financial, operational and improvement performance, including service level agreements

	Technical	People	Scheduling
GM Sales & Marketing	• Recommend to CEO a business development strategy • Develop a branding strategy • Manage stakeholder, government, investor and media relations • Prepare any marketing collateral • Manage events	• Contribute to Executive teamwork on strategy, structure, systems and governance • Lead the implementation of policies and systems in own group • Build and lead a team of direct reports capable of the work • Manage staff performance by setting clear accountabilities and authorities, goals, tasks, coaching, feedback • Undertake manager-once-removed accountabilities for talent management, career planning, succession planning, fair treatment and ensuring competent and consistent leadership at all levels • Work collaboratively across the organisation	• Schedule resources and assign tasks to ensure continuous workflow and fully loaded roles • Monitor and report on group business plans, financial, operational and improvement performance, including service level agreements

WORKS CITED

(n.d.). Retrieved from Beyond Blue: https://www.beyondblue.org.au/the-facts

(n.d.). Retrieved from HeathMath Institute: heathmath.org

(n.d.). Retrieved from https://www.youtube.com/watch?v=nLjFTHTgEVU

(n.d.). Retrieved from https://www.globalwomen.org.nz/assets/Uploads/resources/People-and-culture-resources-The-Diversity-Walk.pdf

Amen, D. (n.d.). Retrieved from American Holistic Health Association: https://ahha.org/selfhelp-articles/ant-therapy/

Amen, D. D. (1999). *Change your brain, change your llife: The breakthrough program for conquering anxiety, depression, obsessiveness, anger, and impulsiveness.* Three River Press.

Bailey, J. (2015). *How To Avoid Being Fired as a Parent: Building Respectful Relationships to Secure your Family's Success and Happiness.* Singapore: Partridge Publishing.

Bolles, R. N. (2016). *What colour is yuor parachute? 2017: A practical manual for job-hunters and career-changers.* Ten Speed Press.

Buckingham, M., & Clifton, D. (2001). *Now, discover your strengths.* Gallop Press.

Centers for Disease Control and Prevention. (2016, June). *Injury prevention & control: Division of Violence Prevention.* Retrieved 09 24, 2016, from https://www.cdc.gov/violenceprevention/acestudy/about.html

Cohen, A. (1993). *The Dragon Doesn't Live Here Anymore.* Ballantine Books.

Collins, D. (2011). *Do you QuantumThink?: New thinking that will rock your world.* SelectBooks.

Covey, S. R. (1989). *The 7 Habits of Highly Effective People.* New York: Simon & Schuster.

Covey, S. R. (2012). *How to Develop Your Personla Mission Statement Quotes* (Com/Cdr Un edition ed.). Franklin Covey on Brilliance Audio.

Dweck, D. C. (2012). *Mindset: Changing the way you think to fulfil your potential.* Robinson.

Engineers Australia. (2016). *The state of the engineering profession .* The Institution of Engineers Australia. Retrieved 09 10, 2016, from https://www.engineersaustralia.org.au/sites/default/files/uploaded/the_state_of_the_engineering_profession_engineers_australia_2016.pdf

Gordon, D. T. (2000). *Perent effectiveness training: The proven program for raising responsible children.* New York: Three Rivers Press.

Harvard Medical School. (2010). *The health benefits of strong relationships*. Retrieved 09 19, 2017, from Harvard Health Publications: http://www.health.harvard.edu/newsletter_article/the-health-benefits-of-strong-relationships

Jaques, E. (1997). *Requisite Organization: A Total System for Effective Managerial Organization and Managerial Leadership for the 21st Century*. UK: Taylor & Francis Ltd.

Jaques, E. (1998). *Requisite Organization: A Total System for Effective Managerial Organization and Managerial Leadership for the 21st Century*. Arlington: Cason Hall & Co.

Kanga, M. (2014). *A strategy for inclusiveness, well-being and diversity in engineering workplaces*. The workplace gender equality agency. Retrieved 09 10, 2016, from https://www.wgea.gov.au/sites/default/files/Inclusiveness_Wellbeing_Diversity_Strategy.pdf

Kanga, M. (2016, 06 05). *Marlene Kanga: women's participation the silver bullet for 'jobs and growth'*. Retrieved 09 10, 2016, from The Mandarin: http://www.themandarin.com.au/66095-silver-bullet-jobs-growth-increasing-womens-workforce-participation/?pgnc=1&pgnc=1

Kay, K., & Shipman, C. (n.d.). *The confidence code: The science and art of self-assurance - what women whould know*. 2014: HarperBusiness.

Kimmel, M. (2015, May). Why gender equality is good for everyone - men included. Retrieved September 8, 2016, from http://www.ted.com/talks/michael_kimmel_why_gender_equality_is_good_for_everyone_men_included/transcript?language=en

Kolk, B. v. (2014). *The body keeps the score: Brain, mind, and body in the healing of trauma.* Viking.

Mills, P. (2015). *Leading people: The 10 successful things managers know and do.* The Leadership Framework Pty Limited.

Mohr, T. (2014). *Playing Big: A Practical Guide for Brilliant Women Like You.* London: Arrow Books.

Pink, D. H. (2011). *Drive: The surprising truth about what motivates us.* Riverhead Books.

Sher, B. (1995). *I Could Do Anything If Only I Knew What It Was: How to DIscover What You Really Want and How to Get It.* Dell.

Sher, B., & Smith, B. (1995). *I could do anything if only I knew what it was: How to discover what you really want and how to get it.* Dell.

Sinek, S. (2011). *Start with why: How great leaders inspire everyone to take action.* Portfolio.

Sinek, S. (Performer). (2013, September 29). *Start with why.* Retrieved September 24, 2016, from https://www.ted.com/talks/simon_sinek_how_great_leaders_inspire_action

ABOUT JENNY

Jenny Bailey is a speaker, author, coach, trainer and consultant, and expert in leadership. Jenny believes that female engineers are 'gold' and make perfect leadership material in the engineering sector. She is the only female leadership coach in Australia with a degree in engineering. She has worked as an engineer and as a senior executive for some of Australia's most respected brands, including KPMG, Rio Tinto, SKM and Yarra Valley Water.

Jenny is described as wise, knowledgeable and compassionate with a structured and logical approach to supporting her clients. She has a knack for quickly spotting the root cause of problems and identifying a practical solution. Her clients often get promoted to better roles within their organisation.

Jenny works with:

- female engineers who want to improve their confidence, effectiveness and work-life satisfaction.

- leaders, in the engineering sector, who are looking for a logical and structured approach to leading high-performing teams.

WORKING WITH JENNY

WHAT CAN YOU DO TO BE THE BEST YOU CAN BE?

Jenny runs the Women in Hard Hats, **group mentoring and coaching program** specifically designed for female engineers. This program comprises eight half-day workshop over a 12-month period and can include one-on-one coaching in order to build mastery and support your career. Contact me at jennybailey.com.au to determine whether this program is for you.

Finally, I'd love to hear your feedback. I'm constantly honing my programs and will be authoring another edition of this book. Please email me, tell me what you liked and what you didn't like, and what you'd like to see more of. Send me an invitation on LinkedIn. You can also register on my website for a fortnightly newsletter that offers career tips and support.

Contact Jenny:
0408 400 659
jenny@jennybailey.com.au

Connect with Jenny:
https://www.linkedin.com/in/jennybailey1/

www.ingramcontent.com/pod-product-compliance
Lightning Source LLC
Chambersburg PA
CBHW060602210326
41519CB00014B/3546